Ancient Pearls of Wisdom

*Learning the Language
of Inner Voice*

Azarm Ghareman, PhD

**Ancient Pearls of Wisdom:
Learning the Language of Inner Voice**

ISBN 9798325791390

First Edition

Printed in the United States of America

Visit www.Mazdaconnections.com

Copyright 2024 by Azarm Ghareman, PhD

All rights reserved. No part of this publication may be reproduced, stored in retrieval system, or transmitted in any form or by any means, electronic, mechanical, photocopying, recording, or otherwise, without prior permission from the publisher.

For
mother who gave me the necklace
and
father who knew they were real pearls.

CONTENTS

Acknowledgements	8
Preface	9
Foreword	10
The Pronunciation of Farsi Vowels	13
Introduction	14
Younger Years	18
Life in the United States	19
A Path Appears	21

PART I   LANGUAGE AND CONSCIOUSNESS — 24

Language as Inner Guide	25
Polarities in the Psyche	28
Dreaming Language	32
Language That Encircles	37

PART II   IN SEARCH OF MOTHER TONGUE — 42

Farsi Language: Figures Embedded Within Words	43
Linguistic Impact of the Arab Invasion	46
Looking for Deeper Roots	50
Journey Takes an Unexpected Detour	52
Reading the Gāthā	55
Translation Pitfalls	57
A Closer Look at the Gāthā	59

PART III WISDOM SPEAKS — 70

The Secret of the Golden Flower	71
Gāthāii: A New, Ancient Word	75
A Commentary on the Gāthāii Intuition of Life	77
Glossary	90
In Case You Have Wondered	102
Sources Consulted	111

ACKNOWLEDGEMENTS

While writing is a private and solitary activity, no one writes a book without the support of friends, mentors, and family. Some of those whom I must thank have already died, but their wisdom has left an indelible mark in my psyche.

My patients, whom I cannot name due to confidentiality, have taken me into their confidence and helped me grow in ways that I could not imagine. They motivate me to listen ever more deeply to their stories.

I thank my daughter Roshan, my siblings, and my friends for their encouragement throughout the process. Anne D'Arcy, sincere thanks to you for reading my manuscript and helping me improve it. We both know that your late husband, Bill Rife, was a mentor to me when I was young and searching for my calling. I wish he were with us to read this book. I'm glad you read it on his behalf.

I am grateful to Dr. Lionel Corbett, Jungian analyst and author, for encouraging me to write. Sometimes a statement as simple as "I think you ought to start writing" plants the seed for a book.

Special thanks to my friend and colleague, Dr. Daniel Snyder, who is a Pastoral Psychotherapist and author in North Carolina. Dan, you spent many hours reading my work, and gave me immensely helpful suggestions. I value our shared interests in language, spirituality, and depth psychology.

Another colleague who deserves my deepest gratitude is Dr. John Lundgren, a Psychiatrist and Supervising Analyst. John, your appreciation for how the psyche communicates through voice and singing is exceptional. Without your voice calling me into my deeper self, there wouldn't be a book.

PREFACE

I have a confession to make.

For nearly 48 years I've felt a quiet guilt within me for not having shared the vicissitudes of life with my compatriots in Iran. I left in 1977. I wasn't there to see how oppressive daily life had become for millions of people; how women were deprived of the basic dignity to shape their own future; how innocent minds became blank slates to be shaped as others wished.

In contrast, I have had complete freedom to read, write, and watch anything that I have wanted. As you will read in the following pages, I have been able to obtain a fine education here in America and grow. Not a day has gone by without me expressing gratitude for this freedom and the fact that no one can control my thoughts and conduct. Not a day has gone by either that I have not been aware of the millions of brothers and sisters who don't have such opportunities. What do I do for them with the gifts of my freedom?

In 2023, when I saw how the voices crying for freedom were brutally crushed in Iran, I vowed that one way or another I would share some of the bounty I have harvested from this land with all those I had to leave behind. From far away, I have tried and will continue to stay connected to the ancient roots of my language and spiritual heritage. I want to share my discoveries with my compatriots hoping that my journey can encourage them to make a similar effort.

This book is also a sincere show of gratitude for the freedoms and opportunities that America has given me. It is my way of paying my debt to life.

San Luis Obispo, California   Azarm Ghareman
February 24, 2024

FOREWORD

This book is for the individual who is drawn to the inner meaning, image, poetry, and the song embedded in a word. Psychotherapists, linguists, immigrants, especially Iranian immigrants, and anyone seeking a path of discovery of one's mother tongue will find reading this book an enriching and rewarding experience.

Dr. Ghareman invites us into her active meditation back to her ancient roots found in her interpretation of the sacred texts of the Gāthā, thus reaching back at least 3,500 years to the beginning of written Indo-European language and its evolution into present Farsi, the spoken language of her country of origin, Iran.

She meditates—dreams—her way into a word to experience how language becomes an inner vehicle for transcendence towards the Unknowable Center. In sharing her journey with us, she shows respect and hospitality for readers of different background by providing careful and succinct "listening posts" as her story unfolds. This enlarges and grounds the concepts she introduces, for example when she talks about Jung. Her writing flows in a simple and playful style, especially as she weaves metaphors throughout the text, but all along she is presenting complex and serious topics and making them accessible to us.

By drawing a parallel with *The Secret of the Golden Flower*, she re-visions the ancient wisdom of the Gāthā, preserved and handed down orally where the text was illuminated by the music of the Gāthā.... a hearing past the literal to living presences who emerge to engage us spiritually and from the depth of our unconscious.

She explores her experience of a primal dialectic, the continual movement between our conscious, literal world of objects and Western language and the inner journey to illuminate the psyche by her embrace of and dreaming the ancient text of the Gāthā, the songs and meditations of Zártosht. As she meditates on a word in the Avesta language, the earliest rendering of the Gāthā, she engages the ancient language of Zártosht and lets it reverberate in her unconscious, a secret light of illumination, of Wisdom emerges. She draws from the meditation on a Farsi word, down and into the ancient meaning and illuminations that reach for but never quite reach the center of the mandala formed by concentric circles. The innermost Center of the circle cannot be known, only sought for. Carefully, she holds the nascent enlightenment, resisting the Western temptation to give it a definition, locate it in a religion and confer an explanation of interpretation. Thus, language for her is a living illumination that seeks transcendence.

In this work, the author explicitly sets apart her journey of the inner expression of transcendent discovery from religion. Her journey carefully frees the essence, the ONE, from "shackles of concrete religion, metaphysics, and the cultural bias" to reveal the timeless essence captured by the meditative path similar to that of The Secret of the Golden Flower. This book is grounded on the meditative exercise on the spiritual soul and primordial spirit in contrast to the material (concrete) sound.

You are invited to journey with and toward your mother tongue and experience the realizations, transcendence and wisdom of your origins.

March 24, 2024   John Lundgren, MD

Remember me?
    I am old. Very old.

        Long before your mother birthed you,
        I was your Mother tongue.

Your people spoke me
I animated their gestures
and moved with their breath
from chest to chest.

        I was the language of dreams
        and the music in their poetry
        I know you've longed for me
        and have grieved me for years

I am not lost; I have not vanished
I am hidden in a cemetery of words

        Look for me; speak me
        and call me into being

I will arise
I will arise!
I am...your Mother!

                                              azarm

THE PRONUNCIATION OF FARSI VOWELS

There are two vowels in Farsi language that are hard to show using the Latin alphabet because there is only the one letter (A) to represent both vowels. This invariably leads to the mispronunciation of many Farsi words.

In some Farsi words, the letter A should be pronounced as the vowel in *fall*, *tall*, or *paw*. I will use **ā** or **Ā** in such cases. For example, Gāthā, or Haurvatāt.

Other times the letter A should be pronounced as the vowel in *apple*, *ladder*, *cat*. These will be written as **á**, or **Á**. For example, Mázdá, Zártosht, Áshá.

INTRODUCTION

A bird doesn't worry about its audience. It starts singing and whoever's window is open will hear its song. That's when I stopped wondering for whom I'm writing this.

My daughter Roshan was about four-years old when one evening she rushed into the kitchen from the backyard and said, "Mommy, the sky is PINK!" "IS IT?" I asked with surprise and went out to see this spectacle with her. Next evening, she repeated, "It's pink again mommy. Why is it pink?" This time she sounded more distressed. What do I tell her? I can't give her the scientist's response to that question and talk about the angle of the sun at sunset, the scattering effect, wavelengths of light, etc. That would have left both of us cold. Instead, we went to the backyard. Looking at the sky I said, "Honey, the sky is pink tonight because pink is the angels' most favorite color!" Roshan smiled and seemed relieved. Never asked me that question again.

This exchange with my daughter is not unlike the questions I've asked myself about life's mysteries and complexities of human relationships. By mysteries I mean ineffable things such as Death, Love, God, etc. for which any answer only deepens the inquiry, like stepping into an endless horizon. They are experiences which seem outside of my control that happen *to* me.

The other set of questions involved daily life decisions we make for which it seemed that answers ought to be more within reach but they were just as baffling to me. How do I know who is a compatible life partner, how to parent a child, or juggle different responsibilities and still have energy left at the end of the day to be approachable for a talk? Would I live my life differently if only a few months were left? What do I owe life? If you've asked yourself similar questions, you are not alone.

For years, I have been searching for a paradigm that would allow me to create *meaning* for what happens in life. Such inquiry seemed especially urgent now, at a time when we humans are tearing each other apart by our ethnic, racial, religious, and political strife and polarity. How do I emotionally survive in the midst of so much chaos? Why are we so cruel to each other? What is the source of evil in the world?

I have always been interested in how religions and various branches of psychology approach the topic of Good and Evil. Explanations for the presence of evil offered by some psychological theories seemed more like excuses to me. I couldn't reconcile any concrete religious beliefs and a laundry list of do's and don'ts with the dream images that were arising from my unconscious. I could not accept that Good and Evil have metaphysical roots. Therefore, the question of what my ethical responsibility toward life and in face of evil in the world ought to be remained unanswered.

In response to these questions that occupied my mind, mythological lullabies, naive psychological theories, and abstract scientific explanations were not satisfying me either. I kept on reading books and listening to lectures. I really tried to apply their tips and insights to my personal life, but truth be told, thoughts of painful past events or fear of future losses continued to creep in and threaten my inner peace. I kept searching for a life intuition, a lens, that could satisfy *all* sides of my mind and meet my intellectual as well as moral standards. Furthermore, even if I find such a lens, is there a language that can adequately convey the richness of that intuition with others without breaking it in the process? I was seeking both—a unifying lens and a language with which to express it.

What I was seeking was not a bigger home, luxury cruise or the latest anti-aging treatment, all obtainable from outside of me. I did not view life as a bucket to be filled either. I was reaching within for something that I couldn't know until I found it. What follows is my attempt to share my inner, self-directed journey for such a lens and language in search for my myth in life. This journey is the culmination of more than 30 years of paying sincere attention to dream images and diligently interacting with as many as I could get a hold of, as well as learning from the lessons that life has required of me. I will share only a few dreams to illustrate how they helped me stay on track at key junctures. I hope that my discoveries, albeit subjective and untransferable, can help you in your spiritual quest and longing.

Our shelves are filled with books about other books. It's as if a book has to reach a certain thickness (spine!) to impress us and be worthy of reading. Many authors cite references nearly on every page. This practice is useful when the writer is seeking academic approval or the reader needs a specific address to locate some information. What I'm writing about can't fit that style. A bee drinks the nectar of many flowers before returning to the hive to make honey. We don't ask the bee, "From which backyard did you get the lavender?" Like a bee, I can't consistently trace my harvest to a specific page and produce a reference in the body of the text. I've been blessed with the nectar of many fine minds to whom I'm forever grateful. What you read now in this spiritual memoir is the honey.

Tears that flow...

   ask the eye

      "Will you mourn us

      when we go?"

                           azarm

YOUNGER YEARS

I was born in Mashhad, Iran, and lived there until age 16. I detested the one-size-fits-all educational system and struggled to fit in and make good grades, which of course I did. I often feigned sickness to stay home from school. One day I overheard my father, who was an internist, tell a friend that he was so distressed by my chronic fever and stomach aches that he was considering taking me to Switzerland for a consultation. That made me feel really bad for the distress I was inflicting on my parents. I soon cured myself from the illness I didn't have and returned to school.

Contrary to the agony of school life, I enjoyed swimming in an internal world that I kept private. I was 12–13 years old when I started saving Persian poems that I liked and copying them meticulously in a notebook. I had no idea that many of these poets were known to the West as luminaries in the world of poetry. To me, they were simply Attar, Mowlavi (Rumi), Hāfez, and many others the West doesn't know. Today I don't think of them as poets only. For me, they are wise, metaphoric depth psychologists. Had I remained in Iran, I would have pursued my passion in Persian Literature or Psychology at a local university. That didn't happen.

My parents were worried about the developing political unrest and my education. Well in advance of the Islamic Revolution, they enrolled me in a private international high school near Geneva, Switzerland. You can imagine how difficult it must have been to watch my childhood home and country recede as I hurried to adapt to a new life and become proficient in French and English. At the tender age of 16, I didn't know how to allow myself to feel homesick and grieve the involuntary loss of my motherland.

What I knew of the world--my language, the poems I loved, customs, values—no longer mattered in the new environment. Survival required that I view and live life differently. Sitting in an 11th-grade Chemistry class, I wondered, "Will there come a time when I can understand everything on the blackboard and copy it before the teacher erases it all?" I knew how hard my father worked in Iran to pay for such an expensive private school. I felt guilty about this opportunity and became even more driven to excel in my studies.

 ## LIFE IN THE UNITED STATES

In 1979, I finished high school and left Geneva for San Luis Obispo, California, to study Chemistry. I thought majoring in Science would require less language proficiency than Liberal Arts. Here was another country to which I must adapt. All that I knew from before receded even farther into the background. When I checked into my assigned locker in the Organic Chemistry lab, the only names on the material list that I recognized were thermometer and matches. That ought to tell you what a steep hill I had to climb. Nonetheless, I obtained a bachelor's degree in chemistry, and later advanced degrees in Chemistry and Business Administration. I studied brain chemistry, pharmacology, consumer behavior—anything that could help me understand the human mind better. I leaned heavily on science for answers. I share this resumé because it's relevant to what comes later in the story. I want you to know that I speak science fluently and respect it as a sharp tool.

After finishing the MBA program, like all my fellow classmates, I looked for a job and was hired by an international consumer product company. I moved to the corporate headquarters in Northern California. My second paycheck hadn't yet been deposited when something in me predicted that, while I could indeed succeed in such a business career, I would eventually perish. To the astonishment of the vice president who had hired me, I resigned and returned home to San Luis Obispo. I felt embarrassed and disappointed in myself for spending eight years in college and graduate school, finishing three demanding programs, and I still didn't know what my calling was. I had remained a driven student who didn't know the difference between getting an A in a class and truly liking the subject matter.

How was it possible that I could take a few drops of an unknown liquid to the lab, run some tests, identify its molecular structure, yet not know the unknown parts that lived in me? Had I adopted the U.S. as my home and become a foreigner to my own nature? Obviously, I did not have answers to these questions. I was not even aware that my academic success in the West was built on a way of perceiving the world through a lens that had gradually alienated me from the world around me and from myself.

Two years passed. It was during this self-alienated phase in my life that my father died suddenly in Geneva from complications of brain surgery. His death shook me to the core and changed the trajectory of my life in ways that took me decades to understand. I became quietly depressed and lost. Somehow, I knew that the time had come for me to find *my* path in life. I yielded to the call.

I cooked, read, wrote poems, stayed still, and listened. Is it too late for me to study psychology—something I had loved from adolescence? The curriculum taught in many psychology programs seemed as nourishing to me as cardboard. I concluded that it probably was too late for me, and that this love would remain unfulfilled. Now what?

A PATH APPEARS

About three years later a good friend introduced me to C.G. Jung's work and encouraged me to apply to specialized programs that focused on his work. I applied; much to my surprise and with no formal degree in psychology I was admitted to a doctoral program in Clinical Psychology. Like a fish thrown back in fresh water, I immediately began to swim.

Even though Jung's language had its own vocabulary, which was entirely new to me (e.g., Objective Psyche, Shadow, Self, Animus, etc.) and drew significantly from mythology and alchemy, there was something nostalgically familiar about his understanding of the human psyche. It's as if I had swum in that body of water before. I couldn't figure out how that could be possible.

Something else occurred during that period which struck me as important: I often walked with a classmate during breaks and discussed what we were studying. When I became frustrated with the limitations of language, I'd resort to reciting a verse from a poem or translating something from Farsi into English. Frequently, both of us would become silent after that. It was as if our urge to communicate had been fulfilled.

For instance, one day he said, "Last night I had a dream that...." I shared with him that in Farsi instead of having a dream we say, "Disháb khāb *didám*" [Last night *saw* a dream]. No, I am not making a grammatical mistake here and omitting the subject (I). I realize that there is no way to render this into English without inserting the subject (I) and separating it from the object (dream). The Farsi perspective implies that the dream image was there before I *saw* it. It wasn't something my brain made at night. Isn't that precisely Jung's point that dream images have their own autonomous reality? We don't create them any more than we create the school bus we see in the street. In the Farsi version there is no need for the subject (I) before the verb. One word does duty for both the verb and the subject. Dreamer is not separated from the landscape and process of dreaming. (This is a glimpse into a nondual language.)

Another example, our class had been studying Jung's concept of the *shadow* and its role in human conflicts between people and nations. "Shadow" is defined as all that a person has no wish to be. We knew just how difficult it is to recognize our shadow let alone own it. I shared with him the Farsi word for neighbor (*hamsāyeh*). (ham=harmonious/equal; sāyeh=shadow). *Hamsāyeh* literally means casting equal shadows. It doesn't suggest I'm identical to my neighbor but implies we cast shadows of equal heights. I don't consider myself superior to my neighbor, nor he to me. How would it impact our neighborhoods and communities if we would extend rights and freedoms to our neighbor that equal what we wish for ourselves? Can an image within a word shift our lens and help us relate to our neighbor as a *hamsāyeh*? Are there words that really do that?

Yes. There are words that do that!

I asked the butterfly,

"Can you read me the writings on the leaves?"

"Do the next thing...," it said.

azarm

PART I

LANGUAGE AND CONSCIOUSNESS

LANGUAGE AS INNER GUIDE

Once I became aware of the unexplored power of images embedded in certain words, language became even more fascinating to me. When people attend silent meditation retreats, there's no talking to one other. They hope that by eliminating distracting speech, they can hear the still *inner voice*. That means a kind of communication is happening deep within them. In what *mode* does the inner voice communicate with us? What is the language of the inner voice?

I wondered if language could fulfil its most essential role as an *inner* guide and beckon us toward a deeper part of ourselves. Can language be used as an inner vehicle for transcendence?

I started paying closer attention to the language we use throughout the day (that linear, one-word-at-a-time way to express thoughts) as well as the language of dreams and images. One day it dawned on me that I had not been hearing any Farsi words in my dreams for a while. Obviously, I had not forgotten how to speak Farsi; what had changed was the lens through which I was viewing the world. That's when I realized the high price I had paid for my so-called successful acculturation.

Apparently over the years while I was learning English grammar and the language of science, both dualistic with clear subject-object delineations, I was unaware of the subtleties and conventions in these lenses that had gradually shifted the lens of how I viewed the world around me.

I wondered if the educated adult in me had joined millions of Westerners whose consciousness, influenced by Western spiritual and philosophical traditions, is characterized by splitting the spiritual from the physical side of life in pursuit of knowledge. Ever since Descartes, there has been an overemphasis on abstract, rational thought. Inevitably, that leads to excess concern with the practical use of external things and external needs, all at the expense of developing our inner capacity for the emotional and intuitive, and somatic ways of knowing. Rational logic is of little help when we face issues that involve emotional conflict or when we search for meaningfulness in life. Furthermore, when we view the world in such a lopsided way, it's as if we are wearing a pair of lenses through which we experience the world in an isolated, interiorized body looking out at an objective world. We have been told repeatedly that only what we see with our anatomical eyes is real. We have been told that "I" am the flesh packed inside my skin and that soul is the result of some neurochemical process in my brain. No wonder aging and death become serious threats to this "I". We have an ambivalent relationship with this isolated and interior "I".

Living with a consciousness that has been so separated, disconnected and split from nature and instincts impoverishes the soul. We can't keep the spiritual pole split from the physical pole forever. The two poles are connected.

Polarities are inherent in the psyche. *Psyche* includes the physical *and* mental. If we ignore the realm in-between—the soul—that connects the physical and the mental, mind becomes as dead as matter, and we'll continue to suffer the consequences of such an artificial split. We say *real* meaning *visible* and *concrete* meaning *material*; we *tattoo* something on our skin instead of living it in an *embodied* way, just to name a few.

Ever so gradually we've lost our way and have suppressed an intuitive way of knowing (i.e., perceiving through other means than our five senses); we outsource our knowing to Apps that tell us how many calories to consume, and whether we slept well the night before. Our devices count our daily steps; even advise a mom an appropriate feeding schedule for her infant. We no longer encounter the world nor participate in it in a soulful way. We are disengaged spectators of life during the day and watch a replay of it on television in the evening. It's hard to overstate how difficult it is to break out of this paradigm. Many of us never break out because we are not aware that we're immersed in it in the first place. If it weren't for our nervousness, addictions, disorientation and health problems sounding the alarm, we may not even suspect that something is wrong.

Everything is

   and

     is not.

       azarm

POLARITIES IN THE PSYCHE

In the last few decades there have been notable efforts in many disciplines to address this psychic split. The popularity of spiritual retreats and books about soul and healing the mind/body split is a testimony to the enormous hunger hidden in the Western psyche for mending the fabric that once connected us to the world. These efforts are indeed necessary, but because they rely mainly on language to shift the paradigm, I believe they face several limitations.

1) It has become fashionable to shun a word and idealize a new one hoping the replacement can carry the freight and solve many of our complex social and cultural problems. That's not going to be enough. Unless we become aware of how the structure of our everyday language (e.g. English) perpetuates the psychic split and shapes the lens through which we fundamentally perceive the world and each other, we deceive ourselves. We'll believe that using this word today and that one tomorrow is enough to heal the split ("We're saving the soul of the world!"), when in reality all we are doing is jumping from one pole of opposites to the other and thinking that we have healed the split.

2) The second obstacle relates to the absence of certain words in a language (e.g. English). I am not talking about words missing in our vocabulary for *things*. Words like contact lenses, smoke alarm, jacuzzi, etc., didn't exist 200 years ago, but once these objects were created and we started using them, their names quickly entered the vocabulary. I'm talking about words that English doesn't have for ideas or concepts (not things) that indeed exist in other cultures and languages. Then what happens? Then a native English speaker doesn't have a *consciousness* for that idea. In other words, if there is no word to

open a crack, consciousness can't find a way to enter. That's when translation calls for a thorough understanding of both cultures and a sensitivity for the nuances within a language.

Translating a word into English when no consciousness for it exists yet in the Western mind can eventually be accomplished, but it would be as slow-moving as painting a mural with a nail polish brush. We are going to encounter a few of these words throughout this book. When you see words like *Nondual, Unlife*, please stay patient for I'm trying to paint a mural for us.

When we talk about a split (as in mind/body split), we are referring to polarity that has gone too far; the tension between the poles has been lost. The split is now a duality. Polarity by itself is not a dirty word. There is a universal tension between opposites. We see this in nature as well as within ourselves or in relationships with each other. Whenever we are repelled by an object or attracted toward it, we are caught up in the drama of the opposites. Just because we're aware that we like or despise something doesn't constitute consciousness. Consciousness means a *simultaneous* awareness of the opposites and an acceptance of that experience. The more we accept that experience, the more conscious we become.

Opposites in the psyche, like in nature, are *complementary*—not contradictory. They balance each other. They show up in the psyche as a pair of two or quaternity. They are *relational*, meaning mutually interdependent. There is no light without shade, no front without back, no male without female, just to name a few pairs.

Our task is to reduce the polarity and reconcile the opposites, not split them even further. We cannot reconcile the polarity of the opposites in the psyche by saying: "Dualism is the wrong view. It's not dual; then it must be all One...we're all one and the same." No! Nondual is not One. It's not Two either. Nondual represents the oneness of two; it represents a shift in the perceptual field. This is an example of the problem of language and consciousness. The structure of a dualistic language such as English makes it hard for nondual ideas to be expressed. Thus, we keep confusing *unified opposites* with an undifferentiated, blended One. Still, we must continue to try and overcome the language hurdle and find a way to introduce nondual ideas to the American consciousness.

Let's take the humble egg as an example: splitting would be separating the egg white from the yolk and putting each in a different saucer. We have just created a duality. Scrambling and whipping the egg makes an undifferentiated, blended mix. We can't tell the yolk from the egg white. The egg, in its original state, is nondual; it has a yolk and egg white but they don't ooze into one another. If you crack the egg open and gently pour the content into a saucer, both the yolk and the egg white maintain their integrity or nondual status. It's worth repeating: The whole egg represents Nonduality. It is not One. It's not Two either.

It would be perfectly legitimate if at this point you say, "Well, if opposites exist in nature and within us, why should we work to close the gap and reconcile them? What's wrong with leaving the polarity be?" And I would say, You are right. There is nothing wrong with polarity. The opposites must initially become separated to create a space for our conscious ego to nestle, but eventually they need to be reconciled or we risk staying divided against ourselves forever. In our current state, we have become *hyperdifferentiated*.

There is an old Egyptian creation myth that shows this process beautifully. It's about Geb the earth god and Nut the sky goddess. They were in a state of union before Shu got between them and pushed them apart. That separated the sky from the earth and created a space for the world to be. The same process takes place in us. Every young ego has to push against that which is pushing against it and create space for itself to be. "I like this one and not that one.... I am this but not that," etc. This is how an individual *shadow* is gradually created in each of us. Shadow is a compost pile of the things we didn't like in us or in others. But sooner or later we have to recognize that the compost pile belongs to us and accept it as an inner reality within us. We are having a heck of a time with this task. In the Western culture the opposites have been shown to us through a lens/language that leaves little choice but for us to feel divided against ourselves—and stay divided. One hand constantly interferes and grabs the other to dominate. That's not Meister Eckhart's teaching of letting go of oneself. We think the compost pile belongs to somebody else, not us. Unfortunately, many other cultures are catching up and copying us in this psychic split just as we're trying to find our way out of this mess.

My quest was a search for a lens and a nondual language through which we can accept, reconcile and unify the opposites on a *higher level of consciousness* without confusing it with an undifferentiated, blended One and risk regressing into the swamp of the Unconscious.

DREAMING LANGUAGE

Earlier I made a distinction between linear languages we use during the day and the language of dreams—images and patterns. Have you ever wondered why we dream in images rather than in our plain, everyday language of logical thoughts and concepts? And why is it important for us to re-connect to the image dimension in our lives?

The original and basic unit of mental functioning is not a thought but the emotionally charged *image*. Psyche doesn't speak English or Swahili—it speaks *image*. The ability to form concepts and thoughts comes later in life. We form concepts through *abstraction*, which is a thought process. As we abstract (Latin *ab-trahere*, to pull away), we pull away our awareness from object and the emotional and psychic reality of the image. Abstraction and objectification distance us from the dream's living reality.

World mythologies have described this activity of consciousness (developing rational thought, conceptualization, repression of emotions) as the creation of the world from original chaos to the establishment of a foothold on dry land to provide safety from the flood waters. We all start out in a state of total identity with this ocean (like an infant). What we call ego development is a gradual separation of the center of consciousness from the world of drives. This process is not only not pathological but is a crucial phase of psychic development as we move from primitive infancy to adulthood.

When this process gets one-sided and we dissociate from our emotions and imaginative faculties, intellect becomes isolated from the world of meaning. Psyche then helps restore the balance by bringing us images expressed in the archaic-symbol language that carry a message of some sort that our one-sided view lacks. In other words, symbols unify the opposites. The unconscious can be reached and expressed by symbols. The symbol is both a wise expression of the unconscious and an idea corresponding to greatest intuition coming from consciousness. Given how cultural-linguistic habits impose limitations on consciousness, psyche, especially as presented in dreams, invites us to participate in a much wider consciousness.

The message that helps restore the psychic balance isn't always palatable and easy to digest. The conscious mind puts up a good fight and resists being drafted against its will. For instance, a soft-spoken woman had a recurring nightmare of someone trying to break into her locked bedroom at night. She'd wake up in fear before there could be any resolution. This woman was active in many volunteer activities, conscientious about the environment and global warming, and she went out of her way to help others and ensure her family's lifestyle didn't hurt anyone or the environment. Her children were well-behaved and exemplary in every way. She had the following dream.

> "I am walking around the local farmers market to buy fresh produce. I notice people are looking at me in a weird way; I look around and see that feces were stuck to the bottom of my shoes which I have dragged all around the food market. It's disgusting. I feel very embarrassed."

For the sake of brevity, I'll share a summary of what her bombshell of a dream revealed. She agreed that something that she had kept locked away from her life was trying to force its way (nightmares) into her awareness. However, it took a long time for her to come around and accept the message coming from her own dream that while deliberately compassionate and considerate in her conscious actions, she was tyrannical and aggressive in her unconscious emotional demands and reactions to people who differed, including her family.

Dream is restoring a balance to her insistence on generating zero waste and the *I-don't-harm-a-fly* attitude by showing that her footprint is anything but carbon-free. After all, how is it possible to exist for one day or even walk one hundred feet without destroying the life of some other creature? Both the nightmare and the farmer's market dream are shadow dreams that ask her to confront her ego-ideal of causing no harm. Reducing environmental pollution has a wider dimension than merely the physical waste we produce. Unless we become aware of how we carry the opposites hidden in the unconscious, we can unleash all kinds of psychic pollutants and emotional viruses into the world.

Recognition of the left-behind part of us (the opposite pole) often creates great psychological tension, as it did for this woman. It's much easier to identify only with one pole, or at the most with one pole at a time. We like the momentum in generates. Conscious experiencing of the hidden opposites without giving in and breaking the tension can be most painful. This can be achieved when we gradually accept the polarity *simultaneously within ourselves*—not one pole at a time. Through curiosity and an inner openness to receive such messages arising from within (dreams) or from without (life), we can cultivate a more collaborative relationship with our unconscious over time.

Now let's return to the question of why the psyche uses images to restore balance rather than making it easier on us by speaking our everyday language? Wouldn't that be more helpful?

We must remember that our consciousness is like a dry land emerged from the vast ocean of the unconscious. The ocean surrounds and contains this tiny dry land, not the converse. The earliest forms of conscious perception happen when our sense perceptions merge into comprehensive images. It's easier to observe this in children: Child points at x, y, z, and parent fills in: "water... fire... or dog." We quickly learn these language conventions and associate *fire* with a thing that heats and burns things. We cannot know what fire really *is* in and of itself because of our limited capacity to experience. We use a string of words to describe fire or anything else for that matter. We distance ourselves from direct experience of life when we construct the world as made up of *outer* objects, which we can name, and when we struggle to master and control our *inner* impulses rather than listening to them respectfully so as to learn from them.

The interesting thing is that the same images that we see in the outer world (water, fire, dog, etc.) are the images the psyche uses to describe the *inner world* and link us back to that emotional world. When we see an image of fire in a dream, we believe it refers to the red, hot thing (bonfire) we made at the beach that evening. We assume the image refers to the outer world even when it arises not from the bonfire but from the inner dimension *like* fire—inner fire: warmth, illumination, enlightenment. We can use a similar example about water. If we dream of water, we assume it's the water we drink or the rain even when the psyche wants to direct our gaze at an inner state *like* water (e.g., Wellspring of life, Fountain of youth, etc.). We are called upon to learn a new way to perceive the inner dimension—*intuiting the inner meaning*. This is a difficult language to learn for many of us because by the time we become aware that there is such a realm as an inner world, we have already established ourselves as rational, solid citizens on the *dry land*; we speak the conventional languages we have mastered; we have severed relation with our inner world and tell our friends: "I had a weird dream."

I discuss the relation of our daily language to dream life in some detail because our everyday language both shapes *and* tracks our consciousness, which in turn influences our dream images and patterns—at least those with a personal

35

dimension. As objects in the outer world change due to our lifestyle, so do the words in our daily vocabulary. My grandmother never saw a bottle of Perrier mineral water in her life. Therefore, her psyche would not have used that image of water to link her back to an inner state. She might have had a dream image of water in a clay pot or a running stream.

Both speaking and hearing are events that are first born in our physical engagement with the world. This is according to the phenomenological view of language. In our earlier example, when a toddler points at an animal wagging its tail, the parent says "dog." As most of us know, the little kid might not say "dog" next time he sees one. He is likely to say "woofie or woof-woof." Good for him. "Dog" is too abstract and removed from the way the child experiences the animal. Of course, the parent corrects and says, "It's a doggie," thinking "doggie" is closer to the child's world, which of course it is not. Depending on the language this child learns to speak, let's say English, some words could continue to sound close to how he'll hear and experience them in the world (e.g., whisper, crack, splash, feather, etc.) but the majority will be a collection of sounds and abstract words (table, lotion, oven, happiness, etc.).

I used to enjoy saying a few words in Farsi to some non-Farsi speaking friends and asking if they could pick the correct meaning simply by listening to the sound. I would say, for example, which word is "song/voice": *zesht, āvāz* or *kootoleh*? They would invariably pick the correct word, (*āvāz*, in this case). Now you can guess how they picked the correct answer. It's as if the word had *flesh*. The sound of the word *āvāz* evokes an image even in the listener who doesn't speak Farsi. The image evoked is that of a mouth open ready to make the sound (ā); the listener's deeper knowing is not intellectual but intuitive. Farsi is one of a handful of ancient languages left in the world that could still connect us to sounds our ancestors once made to communicate. More will be said about this later.

 LANGUAGE THAT ENCIRCLES

Conscious, linear language, that one-word-at-a-time way, however, is limited in what it can evoke in us. Deeper layers of the unconscious can be touched by things such as drawings or artifacts reaching far back in human history. Such things can't be willed or thought up but must appear again as symbols from the forgotten depths if they are to reveal nondual awareness. Earlier I mentioned that the union of the opposites is a process that historically has represented itself in symbols. These symbols can arise from two sources: the unconscious and life itself—if lived with full devotion. In other words, they arise from within or without.

Jung observed that the development of individual personality comes to expression symbolically, sometimes as *personified* figures (not to be mistaken with anthropomorphism), sometimes in images and shapes, and in mandalas.

Mandala means a magic circle in Sanskrit (pronounced mánn-dálá). It's a geometric figure in which a circle is squared or a square is encircled. For the most part, a mandala has regular subdivisions, sometimes four or multiples thereof, and is in the form of a flower, wheel, or cross. They can represent potential for personal or cosmic wholeness. Mandalas are found throughout the world (e.g. Tibetan Buddhism, Christian mandalas, in ceremonies of Pueblo and Navaho Indians) and at times are produced by individuals who feel threatened by inner chaos and fragmentation.

The interesting thing about a mandala symbol is that it is not only a means of expression, but also influences its maker. The mandala image draws an *enclosing circle*, a sacred precinct, of the innermost personality, prevents the outflow, and protects it against deflections through external influences. In other words, the enclosing circle helps bring back the attention to an inner Center. This Center is the place where polarities of Consciousness and Nature arose and where they can become united once again—it represents the nondual One and the ultimate longing of the Soul.

Ancient sages have described this unknowable inner Center in many ways, all of which are still approximations using one abstract word to elaborate on an another one. It's been called *Tao, Atman, It, Tathata, Self, Enlightenment, Mázdá*, etc. When it comes to articulating this unknowable Center, as the Farsi expression says, **"We are a mute with a dream to tell."** The task often falls on gifted poets to express the ineffable, not through prose, but through an image or a metaphor which is really a little poem. A good metaphor can hold the complexity and the tension of opposite poles without breaking it and lead us deeper into a mystery.

The poet Rilke uses the image of moving in *widening circles* and says, **"I live my life in widening circles."** On the other hand, Hāfez (whom I consider the most untranslatable poet of Iran), moves inwardly. He presents the image of the geometric compass used for drawing arcs and circles (*pargār* in Farsi) to describe the process of circulating around a Center. Hāfez says:

> **"Like a compass I am wandering in smaller and smaller circles, never reaching the Center."**

In two short lines, Rilke and Hāfez sigh a longing for that which has occupied the human mind for thousands of years. Can one ever reach the Center and merge with it as medieval mystics longed for? We'll return to this later.

This movement, turning in circles around oneself, when viewed psychologically means involving all sides of the personality. The circular movement activates all the psychological polarities and opposites, light and shade, good and evil, or whatever else the opposites might be. This backward flow or reversal (i.e., realization of the polarity and opposites in the unconscious) is the precursor to the unification with the unconscious laws of being—attainment of that longed-for Conscious life. Wise sages have always known that polarity is what keeps the psyche alive. They have not denied or split them. They've known that opposites have always balanced and complemented one another. Reaching the Center (if we ever can) liberates one from the crucifying conflict of the polar opposites.

God is my centre when I close him in.
And my circumference when I melt in him

I know that without me
God can no moment live.
Were I to die, then He
No longer would survive...

In me is God a fire
And I in Him its glow.
In common is our life,
Apart we cannot grow
                              Scheffler Johannes

Life has not gifted me the talent of representing images that arise from the unconscious by drawing, singing, dancing, or sculpting them. My way is through that mixed blessing of language. I am quite aware of how clumsy our linear language is in expressing the entirety of an experience. Just try to describe to someone, who doesn't know, what lilacs smell like. Or, using words alone, teach someone how to hiccup. You can see how difficult it gets when our linear language, our one-thought-at-a-time way, tries to describe ineffable mysteries such as Love, Death, God, Soul.... It's like trying to grasp water vapor. We'll never know *what* these are in themselves; we can only approximate *how* we experience them.

We seem to have little choice but break this ineffable whole into small enough bits and pieces that we can get a hold of and assimilate one bit at a time (not unlike the scientific method). The unfortunate thing is that we then forget that what we are looking at is only a fragment of the whole that we broke off in the first place. We fail to put it back, so to speak, and we go on throughout life thinking that reality always existed in this cracked, split state. Overspecialization in the field of Western medicine is a good example of how we deal with the complexity of human organism by breaking it into smaller and smaller body parts and then forgetting that this part once belonged to a whole human being.

This limitation of linear language had discouraged me from speaking about ineffable mysteries in prose. A verse of a Persian poem relieved me from that prolonged reluctance:

"Even though we cannot empty the sea with our hands, we can drink enough water to quench our thirst."

The image of making a cup with the palms of my hands to hold enough water to quench my thirst is paradoxical in that it limits—draws a precinct around the vast body of water—

and allows me to hold enough water to take in one gulp at a time. Precisely because a word is limited, it enables me to speak the ineffable one syllable at a time. A word becomes a mandala.

As a word becomes a mandala, Language can fulfill its role as a vehicle to move us toward the Center.

PART II

IN SEARCH OF MOTHER TONGUE

FARSI LANGUAGE: FIGURES EMBEDDED WITHIN WORDS

In this section I would like to take you deeper into the roots of Farsi, with an invitation to notice the many imagistic, emotional, somatic, and deeply personal resonances of language. Our discussion will be relevant regardless of your mother tongue.

The Farsi word for Thought (*ándisheh*) is derived from an ancient Iranian language and means *apparition of a figure* (like Jung's notion of *personifying*). We'll revisit this again later. My personal experience has shown me that by saying certain words out loud in Farsi, something indescribable happens.... It's as if by saying a word and meditating on the meaning of the image embedded in the word, my attention is drawn inwardly toward the core; a self-incubation of a sort takes place.... It's as if I am visiting an old cemetery where figures have been buried within forgotten words. I pause on each gravesite; an image is remembered and a figure is resurrected. I am no longer alone in an objectified world of dead matter. I awaken to a deeper perception in a world that was once alive and is becoming alive again.

For instance, when I eagerly await the arrival of a dear friend whom I have not seen for a long time, I think of the Farsi word for *waiting*, which is *eye on the road* (*cheshm bé rāh*). The root of the word is grown in a linguistic cultural soil that holds a core belief that human experience grows fundamentally out of that in-between world—the Soul. Where are my eyes, really? They are not two isolated circles on my face observing the world; they are on the road awaiting you! The three of us—I, you, the road—form a relational field.... You see how the word pulled me out of isolation and into a relational world? In solitude, I reflect on what I have heard that day in English; I slowly translate some words into Farsi and watch my inner world shift as I am drawn inwardly and embraced by a field that surrounds me. In that experience, I feel distinct and identical, transient and eternal.

Remember me?
   I am old. Very old.

      Long before your mother birthed you,
      I was your Mother tongue.

Your people spoke me
I animated their gestures
and moved with their breath
from chest to chest.

      I was the language of dreams
      and the music in their poetry
      I know you've longed for me
      and have grieved me for years

I am not lost; I have not vanished
I am hidden in a cemetery of words

      Look for me; speak me
      and call me into being

I will arise
I will arise!
I am...your Mother!

                                                                         azarm

Later in the text, we will encounter a few more examples of Farsi words with such gems hidden inside. Farsi is a mine rich in such words. If your mother tongue is not Farsi, you can reflect on the words in your own language, especially in its older or ancient version, and see whether the roots of the words evoke images that lead you to deeper insights.

I have sometimes been asked what led me to such awareness. I didn't set out to arrive at this as a goal. This was not in pursuit of happiness nor a method of self-improvement (we're so fond of turning everything into a goal). As I mentioned earlier, it was my introduction to Jung's writings and his empirical approach that saved me when I was lost in an emotional valley. I had to search and find out from where I had come. Our origins are shrouded in a mystery that is greater than any of our countries of origin or even a linguistic-cultural system. Where we come from, why we are here, how do we navigate the joys and sufferings of life, how to love well … these are fundamental questions that, however buried, lie deep within every heart.

Shortcuts and imitations didn't pay off. Frankly, I didn't know what else to do to climb out of that valley but put one foot in front of the other, and for more than 30 years, work seriously with the material that the unconscious revealed, and do it in the safety of the relationship with my analyst while I raised my daughter, paid the bills and went to work like everybody else.

All along, I remained fascinated with the untapped power of images latent in certain Farsi words and wanted to discover more of them to share with a wider cultural circle, including non-native speakers. I noticed that when working with a patient, every time the moment seemed right for me to share such a word, it opened up a new aperture for the patient to view things differently. Couldn't I have found such words simply by looking at a list of words in a Farsi encyclopedia and selecting the ones that seemed especially soulful? Short answer is no.

When Iranians speak Farsi to each other today, sometimes as many as half of the words they say have Arabic roots. This is not just due to the Islamic Revolution in 1978-79. The roots go much further back in time to the Arab conquest of Iran (630+ AD), which inflicted a deep wound in the Persian psyche. Invading Arabs who had never seen books burned libraries and countless irreplaceable manuscripts. Anything and anyone who opposed their ideology had to be destroyed. They were determined to use the power of the sword to impose Islam on Persians and cut them off from their cultural and spiritual heritage.

LINGUISTIC IMPACT OF THE ARAB INVASION

Persians at the time of the Arab conquest (630+ AD) spoke *Pahlavi* (or *Middle Farsi*, derived from Ancient Fasi), and they practiced an altered form of Mázdáism (Mázdáism=Zoroastrianism). Because much of the religious Mázdean teachings were recorded and shared in the Pahlavi language, you can understand why the invading Arabs were determined to destroy Iran's main language. It is easier to dominate a group and impose a new ideology when people are deracinated from their culture and language. Sadly, it wasn't only Arabs who participated in this linguistic annihilation and cultural assault; many converted Iranians were just as zealous.

Unlike the Egyptians who fully surrendered and adopted Arabic as a result of the Arab Conquest, thus losing their own language and breaking the continuity with their great civilization, Iranians resisted and never fully adopted Arabic.

While they did lose their language of that time (Pahlavi), another Iranian language (*Farsi Dári*) from east of Iran replaced it. Today Iranians speak Farsi Dári into which many, many Arabic words have infiltrated. There are dozens of other Iranian languages still spoken in Iran, but Farsi remains the main and common language binding the citizens together.

The following table shows the languages we've been discussing in a more organized way. It'll be a helpful reference as you read about dates and names of unfamiliar languages.

Table 1

Farsi is an Indo-European language, like English, French, Greek, etc. There are about 450 Indo-European languages that are divided into various branches. One of them is the Indo-Iranian branch (>300 languages) which is further divided into:

Indo-Aryan languages (about 220—Sanskrit, Pali, Vedic Sanskrit, Nepali, etc.) and

Iranian languages* (about 100)

*The Iranian languages in turn are classified into three groups, based on time periods where the language underwent the most significant changes.

Ancient Iranian Languages	Middle Iranian Languages	New Iranian Languages
(1700–1500 BC to 300 BC)	(400 BC–1400 AD)	(1400 AD–present)
• Avesta (Eastern parts of Iran) • Ancient Farsi (Western part of Iran) • Ancient Pārti • Mādi • Sákāi, etc.	• Pārti • Soghdi • Pahlavi (Pahlavi is derived from Ancient Farsi) • Sákāi, etc.	• Farsi Dári • Loree • Kordi • Āzári • Pashtu • Pamiri • Baloochi, etc.

47

I must emphasize that I have no wish to undervalue Arabic or any other language, nor do I wish to revitalize Farsi to soothe a cultural nostalgia. Although Arabic's aggressive intrusion into Farsi was not an organic exchange that normally happens between related languages over time, Farsi doesn't have to remain chained to Arabic. I agree with those who say that modern Farsi, still a live Indo-European language, can fortify itself in today's rapidly developing scientific world and create *new* words by drawing from several resources such as its own ancient linguistic roots, other languages spoken within Iran, or by borrowing from other languages in the Indo-European family.

Ever since the Arab conquest (630+ AD), so many Arabic words have flooded the Farsi vocabulary that many Farsi words and basic verbs have been essentially eclipsed and forgotten. In my opinion, one of the most damaging consequences of this linguistic intrusion is felt in the psyche. The images that were embedded in those Farsi words are now being blocked from the Iranian psyche. Over the centuries, Iranians have become *culturally homeless* regardless of whether they are living in Iran, Europe, or the United States.

Home is not only *place*; it is also psyche's native habitat in language and culture. An invaded and dominated people, as well as a displaced or enslaved people, are forced into a cultural-linguistic diaspora. Cultural homelessness is not just emigrating to another country. It's being cut off from images that once spoke to our ancestors and gave life meaningfulness. In experiencing such a psychic split, Iranians share the same fate as millions of Tibetans, Celts, as well as African and Native Americans.

Are you beginning to wonder what this discussion about Farsi language or cultural homelessness has to do with you? After all, you may be a Westerner with no need for Farsi or even a second-generation Iranian who is speaking English like a native and gets by just fine with the Farsi he knows.

As I showed in Table 1 (page 47), Farsi is one of the oldest languages in the world and belongs to the Indo-European family of languages with roots in Roman, Germanic, Celtic, Greek, Armenian, Albanian and Baltic-Slavic cultures. So, it's not as unrelated to English as it seems. When a Farsi word is forgotten, completely lost, and the image is blocked from consciousness, it's being blocked for millions of us, not just Farsi speakers.

Here's an experience I had in the clinical setting that shows how the act of deeply listening to someone's language and seeing the images embedded in it can open up an inner path.

I once worked with an American professional whose chief complaint was lack of joy in life and in his marriage in particular. One day he brought a dream that he quickly brushed aside saying, "Probably means nothing...makes no sense." This dream consisted of one image. It just happened that as he said the name of that image in English, it sounded like a suffix in some ancient Farsi words that I had learned. Not knowing what else to do with that image, I took that path and *translated* his dream image into Farsi and then back into English for him. I said, "The image in Farsi means something that's condensed and encapsulated. Maybe your dream is giving us a picture of just how tight and depressed you feel internally."

What happened next was wordless. He closed his eyes, took a breath and exhaled deeply. Then opened his eyes and smiled. He heard the dream's invitation to depth.

 **LOOKING FOR DEEPER ROOTS**

I am not the only one advocating that Iranians incorporate more Farsi words in their language instead of Arabic-derived. Scholars have discussed this and efforts have been made to create new words or bring back some of the authentic Farsi words into circulation. (See the section called In Case You have Wondered). However, as I have shown, modern Farsi has many tributaries. I needed to do some linguistic archaeology in order to get past the barriers that a linguistic imperialism had imposed on my soul. I have looked at several resources that had long list of words rendered back in Farsi. I found them quite helpful, but I couldn't hastily memorize the list without going through the process myself. I wanted to carefully compile a list of everyday words in Farsi and gradually and organically weave them into my conversations.

I spent months generating a list of about 2500 common words that were Arabic-derived and rendered them back into Farsi. Next, I alphabetized the list and made a sentence with each Farsi word, thinking it will make it sound more natural if I learn the word in the context of everyday conversation. Of course, that took even longer because in the process of building a sentence and incorporating more words, I faced the earlier hurdle. Is *that word* Arabic-derived or Farsi? You can see why the process was so time consuming. I had to remain patient and learn from the process before sharing it with others.

Later, I read and recorded each sentence as voice memo in my phone. Just as years ago I had memorized a long list of French or English words in high school, I kept repeating the new Farsi words aloud while walking or doing chores at home. These were not Farsi words I had forgotten due to emigration to Switzerland in 1977; these were words from a nondual language that Iranians had lost in the last 1400 years.

Initially it seemed straightforward to recognize the lineage of a word. That fantasy soon came to an end. Sorting out whether a word has Farsi or Arabic roots was like someone asking me to separate salt from pepper granules that have been thrown in a big pile. What made the process so challenging? Here is an example. I thought *eshgh* (meaning love) is for sure Arabic because there are several other Arabic derivatives stemming from it (e.g., *ashegh, mashoogh...*). Even the reputable Dehkhoda Encyclopedia said *eshgh* has Arabic roots, but after learning what other scholars had carefully researched, I learned that the roots of *eshgh* go all the way back to Avesta language (an Ancient Iranian language (see Table 1, page 47) and other Indo-European languages.

This word was adapted by Arabic, which replaced some of the letters, then returned into the Farsi vocabulary along with several Arabic cousins and relatives. That's why I couldn't hastily pick up a ready-made reference book from the shelf without questioning the author's meticulousness. I opted to educate myself about the history and evolution of the Farsi language and Iran's rich mythology using multiple sources for comparison. My science background became a helpful ally during this phase, for I had to call upon disciplined patience, focus, and critical thinking and not be misled by a writer's exaggerated sentiment, or ethnic and religious arrogance. My own emotional response to what I studied had to be equally monitored in the process.

JOURNEY TAKES AN UNEXPECTED DETOUR

The example I shared (*eshgh*) created a conflict within me and brought my search to a standstill. I debated whether I should continue compiling more Farsi words the way I had been and proceed to share what I had with others online or pause and learn more verbs/words in Avesta to help me trace the lineage of words when in doubt. You see, if the root of a word I'm looking at is Avesta, then that word isn't Arabic based.

Learning Avesta sounded good in theory except that apart from a few Avesta scholars who know the language intimately, Avesta is not a living language. Furthermore, did that require me to revisit Mázdean (=Zoroastrian) religion and mythology? I had enthusiastically studied Mázdáism for my doctoral dissertation about 30 years ago and showed it to be an ancestor of Archetypal psychology, but the material didn't hold my psychological interest for more than a few years. That was not the lens I was looking for. I kept coming back to Jung and his empirical findings about the psyche because they resonated with images arising independently within me. At times I felt unfaithful to what I thought was my spiritual heritage, but I had to remain true to myself and keep on searching for a different lens.

If nearly every Iranian, even if a devout Moslem, knows that his spiritual heritage prior to Islam was Mázdáism, then what was my reluctance about? Open any book or article about Mázdáism and you'll read about the struggle of good and evil, ideas of heaven and hell, and how the ideas of Zártosht (the Farsi name for Zoroaster) have influenced Abrahamic religions as well as Buddhism. You'll meet Ahriman (Satan) pinned against Ahura Mázdá (Christ) until the end of the world when a savior restores peace and justice.

As I mentioned at the beginning of the book, for years I have been interested in how religions and psychology approach the mystery of Evil in the world, and how I have been searching for a spiritual perspective, a lens, that would help me make sense of today's world and our fragmentation. I couldn't reconcile these Mázdean nor any other concrete religious beliefs with the images arising from dreams and my unconscious. For the life of me, I could not endorse the disastrous hypothesis that there is an Absolute conflict in this world between Good and Evil that can never, ever be reconciled and harmonized. I could not accept Good and Evil are rooted in metaphysics. You can see why I felt conflicted about learning archaic Avesta words in the context of Mázdean teachings. The conflict wouldn't let me move forward or be settled by my will and logic. Again, I had to wait and trust the process. About a month later help came from two dreams a few weeks apart.

Dream 1
A woman tells me she knows how to polish pearls by gently sandpapering them. I asked if she'd teach me. I tell her my mom gifted me a pearl necklace, three strands, that had been given to her at her wedding. (It's true. I took the necklace to a jeweler in 1980s to be rethreaded and triple twisted into a shorter, more modern-looking necklace.)

Dream 2
I'm looking in the mirror that recalls my mother's bedroom vanity. I'm holding a bridal bouquet and it's presumed that I'll be walking down the aisle. What I'm holding is a plain ivory color clay figurine mounted on an ivory color base with her hands on each side and palms open. A few flowers surround her. Is this a baby, a woman, or an angel? All that outlines her contour is a small purple flower in each hand and maybe a tiny purple flower for earring. Will the guests know what I'm holding? I say to myself if I color her lips purple then she'll look even more like a human, but I don't because I don't want to turn her into a doll.

Briefly said, my task was to gently uncover the face of something old and precious that I had been endowed with and remove the tarnish that has been accumulated over time so what lies underneath can emerge. The necklace represents a legacy gift that must be re-threaded and brought into my present life.

I thought the figurine represented the archetype of the Eternal Feminine, Holy Wisdom, Soul, Sophia. The dream had situated her in my parents' bedroom in my native land. Who was she to me? It took a lot more exploration into ancient Iranian and other Indo-Aryan mythology and spiritual practices before the face of this figurine emerged in a culturally relevant way for me. Her name is *Armáiti* (pronounced Armá-y-ti). We'll come back to her later.

Tension within me eased. I knew I was headed down the path (marriage aisle) that represented my journey of bringing the opposites together—the secret magical process which produces the child. I experienced this as accepting my psychological destiny. I was required to slow down, go way back in time, and learn key Avesta words and verbs.

The journey that I had started and thought was in search of reviving Farsi words suddenly took a detour and became very serious. Life turned quiet. I knew I was alone on this part of the journey because it was my path, my life, my responsibility to complete. No one else could do it for me. I couldn't stop being pulled deeper within.

READING THE GĀTHĀ

Not knowing where to start learning Avesta words, I remembered I had seen Avesta alphabet in some books I had in my bookshelf. Of course, I didn't know how to read that alphabet. I picked up the two thick volumes called the *Gāthā* that had been sitting there for more than 30 years (pronounced *Gawt-hah*; plural of Gāt, meaning poems, chants). These had been gifted to my parents in their last trip to Iran shortly before my father died in 1990. The author of the two volumes (Azárgoshasb), an Iranian scholar in Avesta and Mázdáism, had spent many years of his life translating the Gatha word by word from Avesta language into Farsi. He presented the translations and interpretations of four or five other Iranian or world scholars in addition to his version. He then restated each verse in Farsi in a free-flowing style to make it more accessible to contemporary Iranians. That seemed like a good path for me to take.

Background

The word *Avesta* is used in two ways. It either refers to one of the Ancient Iranian languages (1700-1400 BC), see Table 1, page 47), or to the name of the book of what is known today as Mázdean religious teachings. Like the Bible, the book Avesta has been assembled and has several sections written at different times throughout history, some after the Arab conquest. Today's Avesta book is a collection of five parts (Yasna, Visparad, Vendidad, Yasht, and Khordeh or little Avesta). Yasna section consists of prose and poems. The poem part is known as the Gāthā (chants = *Gita* in Sanskrit) that are dispersed throughout the Yasna, making up a total of 16 sections (28-34, 43-46, 47-50, 51). Some researchers consider section 53 as a part of the Gāthā also, thus making a total of 17 sections (see Glossary).

Other than the Gāthā, none of the other sections of Avesta book are based on the original teachings of Zártosht. None.

After Alexander's invasion (334-326 BC), the Arab conquest (630+ AD), and the Mongol invasion (1258 AD), countless manuscripts and records were destroyed and had to be re-recorded. Over time, different dynasties and groups in power inserted the interpretations, translations and beliefs that suited their motives and beliefs. For instance, the *Moghs* were a powerful priestly clan at the time of the Achaemenid Empire and amongst the Medes in northwest Iran (Medes ethnically are today's Kurds). Their influence fluctuated depending on the dynasty in power. After several centuries when Zártosht's teachings had already been compromised by the clergy in the eastern part of Iran, the Moghs from the western part created a concoction, reintroduced many of their old Aryan practices that Zártosht had strongly rejected, and presented it as Zártosht's teachings. They brought back old Mithraic beliefs, burial customs, ritual animal sacrifices, ancestor worship, and worship of elements such as fire. For the confusion surrounding the term *mogh*, see the section "In Case You have Wondered."

Today what most Iranians (including many academicians) know as Mázdáism and the Avesta book is a far cry from the original. The teachings are twisted-beyond-recognition, a nearly opposite version of Zártosht's original teachings. Regrettably, it is the altered version of Zártosht's teaching that found its way to the West and misled many scholars and writers, including Voltaire and Goethe, who associated Zártosht with sorcery and magic. Finally, in the 18th century, a French linguist noticed that the language in some parts of the book of Avesta was strikingly different from the rest of the text. The language of that part was similar to Sanskrit but several centuries older than Sanskrit, which suggested that those parts were much older than the rest of the text.

It is only in the last 200 years, through the intense work of comparative linguists and researchers, that new light has been shed on those parts of the Gāthā that are distinct from other sections of Avesta that had obscured it. That's when the passion grew more intensely both within and outside Iran to understand the message of the original text more deeply.

I am sorry to say that my own dissertation was based on references and resources that, as I see now, relied on the new Avesta (what I call the adulterated version). I didn't know about any of these discrepancies until a year ago when I picked up the two volumes of Gāthā. Even then, I thought I was going to learn a few new Farsi words here and there— I had no idea that what would emerge in the process would affect me to the core.

 TRANSLATION PITFALLS

When I started reading the word-by-word translation and interpretations of the Gāthā (Āzárgoshasb's or other translated versions), I was keenly aware that I am at the mercy of someone else's understanding of what an ancient Avesta word (3500–3700 years old) means today, even if that someone is a world scholar whose translations sound beautiful. A comparable example of what I am saying applies to Sanskrit, the sacred language of India, especially Vedic Sanskrit, which shares common roots with Avesta (although Avesta is an older language). Neither Indian nor other world scholars can be sure of an exact translation, and many modern dictionaries are forced to rely on a single source, which is a lexicon compiled by Böthlingk and Roth in latter part of 19th century and is known to incorporate a good deal of guesswork.

You can see how this would affect a reader's understanding of the Vedas and Upanishads. As a motivated student, I had to be vigilant about the pitfalls of arbitrary translations of a word which would reduce Gāthā to yet another philosophy or religious text. I view the Gāthā as a way of *Liberation* from such straitjackets.

Here's a good example to show just how carefully I had to proceed at this point on the journey so as to avoid drawing hasty conclusions. The word *Mázdá* is made of *máz* (big) and *dá* (knowledge/wisdom, which also can refer to the verb giving, growing). So, *Mázdá* means Supreme Wisdom (Big Mind) or Grower of Life. When a Gāthā translator says that *dá* means "to grow or to create," as if these verbs are interchangeable in this particular context, is he aware that he has just inserted an entirely different lens through which his reader is invited to see his relation to the world? There is a vast difference between a *grower of life* and a *creator of life*! Do you see how a word just carelessly slipped in? If *Mázdá* is translated as a Creator of Life, then I as a human would be a creature created by a God. We're back to the stepwise, carpentry model of the world of Abrahamic religions in which I am separated from The Maker, thus needing all kinds of intermediaries (churches, mosques, buildings, prayers, sacrifices, repentance, clergy, Holy Spirit, priests and rituals) to overcome the distance.

This is a perfect example of how a translator's bias is imported into the translation. *Mázdá* refers to a nondual field of perception, and the translator has distorted it by placing it under a subject/object lens.

It gets even more treacherous when the translator slips in *father* as a synonym for what he had just assumed was the Maker of the world. He may not be conscious of the extent to which the Abrahamic religions are influencing the lens through which he sees the words he translates. By reading the translated text, I did not know whether Zártosht (3700-3500 years ago), right or wrong, meant *Mázdá* as grower or creator of life. Zártosht is dead, and I can't get clarification directly from him. I had to suspend judgement and try to avoid making any assumptions. I could only intuit his intention after reading the Gāthā in its entirety.

A CLOSER LOOK AT GĀTHĀ

Who is Zártosht and what are the Gāthā about?

There is no shortage of debate about Zártosht's background, when and where he lived, and his message. Some have a strong need to mythologize or historicize him. I am not interested in participating in philosophical debates, for I am neither a religion scholar, a comparative mythologist, nor a linguist. I present a general outline about Zártosht's date/location that has made sense to me after reading many points of view, and I prefer to focus more on the content of Zártosht's teachings and their relevance for us today. Highlighting the approximate date matters because it makes us value even more the depth of his insights so far back in history.

Some writers, not spared from political motivation or envy, get excited to *prove* that their land was where a particular poet or prophet originated or an ancient artifact was discovered. I think that is like saying, "The sun rose this morning in our country. We saw it first...it's ours." We all see the sun at different times of the day, and though its light appears differently and we use different words to describe it, we're talking about the same sun. Same mysteries have perennially awed and perplexed humans of all ages: ancient as Zártosht, Siddhartha, Jesus; recent as Jung, Einstein, Rilke, Emerson, Hāfez; and young as the four-year old astonished by "the PINK sky."

What follows is a brief discussion of important points that I have learned about Zártosht and the Gāthā.

1) It is now believed that the migration of Aryans, so named because of their proximity to the Aral Sea, began to migrate from the area just north of Afghanistan about 2,000 BC. This was not a single event but happened over time and in several stages. Some began to migrate toward India and Iran (both the eastern and western parts) about 1,700 BC and reached the Indus River. For the purpose of our discussion, it's important to note that prior to migrating toward Iran and India (1,700 BC), these people lived near each other and shared a common language. Their languages (Vedic, Gāthāii) have many similarities, even some identical words. Zártosht most probably lived sometime between 1700 BC and 1400 BC, during the Bronze age, somewhere near the Aral sea among ancestors of the Aryans who later migrated toward Iran and India.

Researchers rely on three types of resources to estimate dates for Zártosht and the Gāthā.

- Historical documents and writings of Roman or Greek historians
- Anecdotes and stories
- Linguistic and archeological comparisons

Based on the range of opinions that I have read, the linguistic comparisons are less subject to bias, thus a more reliable indicator of the date of Gāthā. Due to their linguistic similarities, if ever the age of the Vedas is revised, the age of the Gāthā needs to be revised accordingly. Until then, a convenient way to remember all this would be to say that Zártosht and the Gāthā are about **3,500 to 3,700** years old.

2) If Zártosht indeed lived near the Aral sea in central Asia amongst ancestors of the Aryans who later migrated toward

Iran and India, this suggests he had never even stepped into where Iran is today; therefore, it may be more accurate to refer to him as an ancient (Aryan) sage with a universal message than claim him as Iranian and draw a narrow geographical border of existence around him.

3) Unlike the Upanishads, which are authored anonymously, the Gāthā are chants directly composed by Zártosht in an archaic dialect (Gāthāii, or Gathic) and passed on orally until they were compiled and recorded later. Sometime between 300 and 400 AD, the Avesta alphabet was created to copy the sounds and phonetics of the songs of the Gāthā. It is considered one of the most precise alphabets in the world.

Zártosht clearly was an individual who made references to personal experiences, even to his daughter's wedding and the advice he gave the young couple. From the choice of words used in the Gāthā, we get the impression that Zártosht was an ordinary man who did not rise from a privileged or priestly class. He was against the priestly clan of his time and the demands they made of the people. He lived long before society was divided into workers, farmers, soldiers, and royalty.

4) The influence of Mázdean teachings can be detected in Mahayana Buddhism (more so than in Theravada Buddhism) and in Taoism. It's a documented historical fact that northwestern parts of the Indian subcontinent were under the control of the first Persian Empire (600–400 BC). When Mahayana doctrine was being created, an Iranian tribe with their Mázdean faith established a kingdom in northern India. Their king Kanishka, who engaged top Buddhist scholars of the time, is essentially responsible for creating the Mahayana doctrine.

The Mázdean influence spread far beyond India. Many of the missionaries who carried Buddhism into central Asia through the Silk Route were ethnically Iranian. Keep in mind that at this point in history about 1,000 years have passed since the time Zártosht lived, and many of his teachings that reached India may have already been distorted.

From my perspective, the message of the Gāthā is far more present in Taoism than in Mahayana Buddhism. As you may know, Taoism is the original Chinese way of liberation that later combined with Indian Mahayana Buddhism to produce Zen. In the process of evolution of Asian thought, Zártosht's teachings that had been imprisoned may have become liberated again in Taoism. No wonder the essence of the Gāthā is reflected more in Taoism than Buddhism.

5) I am not quite sure why a parallel spiritual liberation hasn't happened in the evolution of God image in the dominant forms of Christianity and Islam. If anything, the God image became even more split (Merciful Allah against Satan). Maybe geopolitical and economic factors in the Middle East play a role. When people talk (boast?) about the influence of Zártosht on Judaism, Christianity, and Islam, and think that they are tracing ideas of hell/heaven, monotheism, etc. to Mázdáism, I am convinced they are influenced by the new (adulterated) Avesta, not the original teaching as expressed in the Gāthā. As you'll see, neither monotheism nor dualism apply to the vision of life in the Gāthā. In my opinion, *Non-dual* describes the Gāthā best.

6) A point that's often overlooked is that throughout the Gāthā, Zártosht not even once claims that his teachings are direct words of God. These chants are reflective of an intimate relationship and longing with his Source. He does not see the divine in a burning bush or ascend to the sky. It's through inner search and an evolving inner dialogue that Zártosht comes to this intuition of life. He considers himself an initiator of a lifelong learning process and urges us to reflect and find our own unique path in life. Expecting that we follow him or anyone else as a guide forever is not his hope either. (This reminds me of Jung saying, "Thank God I'm Jung and not a Jungian.") No wonder that initially there were no religious buildings or fire temples, no statues, no rituals, no need for intermediaries such as priests to claim they can help us get to heaven. All such obstructions appeared later.

7) Contrary to common belief, there is <u>no</u> connection between the message of the Gāthā and Mithraism, Zurvanism, or Manichaeism (see Glossary). Prior to Zártosht, Aryans believed in natural elements and multiple gods (Mithra, Indra, Varuna, Agnes, etc.). Zártosht rejected all forms of anthropomorphism, formalized rites and concretized mythology. He neither names nor directly attacks a revered Aryan deity and, consequently, redirects the discourse away from them. After Zártosht, however, many earlier Aryan practices such as Mithraism were reintroduced by the *Moghs*, as was Zurvanism.

Fire is mentioned half a dozen times in the Gāthā but not as a separate entity to be worshiped; fire symbolizes consciousness and provides a focal point for one's inner gaze. Light of the fire should not be mistaken with the light that shines but Light as world Principle, the positive pole.

8) There is nothing metaphysical about the Gāthā. Zártosht doesn't speculate what happens to us after we die; he doesn't say whether we merge and dissolve in God or not. He offers no anticipation of Heaven or Hell after death. The words used in the Gāthā for what we call heaven or hell today represent *internal* states that we create during our lives as consequences of our individual thoughts, words and actions. In fact, the Avesta word for the internal state known as Heaven is *Garo demana,* which means *abode of songs.*

9) Contrary to many interpretations, the Gāthā don't say that Good will prevail over Evil. Nor do they say that followers of Zártosht will prevail at the end. What they say is those who align their thoughts, words, and actions with the natural rhythm of life will prosper, meaning they can reach an internal state of fulfillment.

There is no mention of an apocalypse, no day of judgement, no resurrection, no reincarnation, no savior to rescue us, nobody to bribe in exchange for forgiveness, and no winged angels. Zártosht's message is about experiencing life here and now. On this point he reminds me of Jung, who remained disciplined and refrained from speculating about the unknowable, about which nothing can be determined. (Jung cautioned us not to mix up our self-enlightenment with the light of the S̲elf. I'll return to this important point later. S̲elf was the term he used for the totality of the psyche; see Glossary.)

10) We are encouraged to experience life mindfully and joyfully in relationship to nature and to the community at large. Now that requires a lot of emptying of our minds from many of the teachings that came later and created a dualistic division of spirit as good and body/matter as bad. For Iranians especially, it also requires a lot of emptying of the minds from many post-Islamic indoctrinations of martyrdom and wailing for religious figures who died centuries ago.

11) You may remember that in our discussion about mandalas, I mentioned that the unknowable inner Center has been given many names: *Tao, Atman, It,* etc. Zártosht selected **Mázdá** to represent that which exists by itself.

Mázdá means Grower of Life, also Supreme Wisdom. Some writers have rightly pointed out that a word is sometimes used in the Gāthā as an adjective, but that adjective gets stuck to a name and eventually people think the adjective/

name is the real name. One important example is the adjective *Ahura,* which means nourisher or giver of life (common root with Vedic Asura). So, *Ahura Mázdá* in the Gatha is an adjective/noun and literally means *Grower of Life/Wise*. It flows better if we flip the order and say Wise Grower of Life. The name for the unknowable Center is *Mázdá,* not Ahura Mázdá!

The adjective adds some definition to the noun. However much we might be drawn to adjectives such as *wise,* or even *loving* or *infinitely compassionate,* they still tend to objectify the unknowable Center, that which is beyond all words. Thus, Ego is forever trying to grasp that which cannot be grasped by words, and in doing so we objectify that which lives beyond all subject/object dualities.

If you come across a text that refers to Ahura Mázdá as one entity, you know the writer is influenced by the new Avesta.

12) Another distortion in the new Avesta, equally important to note, occurs when the six *aspects* of Mázdá presented in the Gāthā are turned into six Archangels and presented as separate entities called *amesha spenta* (Holy Immortals). The six aspects are indeed mentioned in the Gāthā but never as a group nor as separate, concretized figures the way they are portrayed and anthropomorphized in the new (adulterated) Avesta. The words *amesha spenta* are never mentioned in the Gāthā, yet scholars and translators continue to give lectures and write books about them as if they were.
The six aspects of Mázdá in the Gāthā are the following:

- **Vohu Mana**
- **Áshá**
- **Khshathra**
- **Armáiti**
- **Amertat**
- **Haurvatāt**

I realize these six words are abstract and mean nothing to you at this point. I hesitate to give a quick translation for these important words. The valorization of Gāthā has suffered enough because of cursory translations. I will introduce them in the section called "A Commentary on the Gāthāii Intuition of Life." The six aspects of *Mázdá* represent a net of jewels in which every jewel contains the reflection of all the others.

13)   In addition to the six words mentioned above, there are a few additional terms in the Gāthā that are essential to the understanding of the ancient text's esoteric meaning but are untranslatable. Scholars have presented their interpretations of the verses based on their own understanding, but there can be no true equivalent in today's language when there is no longer an experience of it in our lives, and therefore no consciousness of it.

Let's remember that it's only in the last 200 years that the scholars have taken a closer look at the deeper meaning of the Gāthā. That's more than 3,500 years since Zártosht and after centuries of the text being forced into the mold of the *ideological* teachings of Abrahamic religions, all of which have a split God image (Good God, Evil Satan). Thankfully, mystical sects have always thrived underground.

It's very difficult to recover from such influences and see beyond the lens they place on us. We are badly in need of a language that retrieves the original meaning which has been obscured probably in all sacred texts of the world.

Following are some of the key Avesta words from the Gāthā to illustrate my point.

- *Mainyu* is from the infinitive *man*, meaning to think or meditate. It's invisible and related to the mental and spiritual. *Mainyu* is the complementary pole to *Gaethya*.

- **Gaethya** has been related to the earth and translated as the Material world. *Gaethya* is the complementary pole to *Mainyu*.

I see it as related to the terrestrial and the sensible realm; that which has *Form*. The ancient East did not start from the same point of departure as many parts of the West by dividing the world into Mind and Matter; rather, it's Mind and Form.

- **Vohu** has been nearly always translated as Righteous, Right, Good. **A big misunderstanding of the Gāthā caused by inadequate translation starts here!** The Farsi word for following straight along a path (*rāst*) also happens to mean Right as in Just and True in a moral sense. Interpreting this crucial word in such a narrow way reduces the Gāthā to abstractions of rational and rationalist morals, commonplace enough to fit anywhere. Although such abstractions and moral rationalism do not at all fit Zartosht's intuitions.

Vohu is that which follows the Way; it goes with the suchness of things; it is in harmony with the rhythm and Laws of the Universe. That's it. Vohu should not be narrowly interpreted as Right over Wrong.

- **Akem** has been translated as wrong, bad or a lie. No! Akem represents the complementary pole to Vohu, not contradictory to it. Akem is that which is not along the path or not in harmony with Laws of the Universe.

- **Spenta** has been translated as Beneficial, Pure, Holy. I read it as something that is continuously moving toward that which is in harmony with the rhythm and the laws of universe. It's an adjective and should not represent a concretized, separate entity. Spenta Mainyu would roughly mean a *Spirit Continuously moving toward Harmonizing*.

- **Angra** is the complementary pole of Spenta. It, too, is an adjective and should not represent a separate figure. So, Angra Mainyu would roughly mean a *devolutionary, disharmonizing Spirit*.

Wherever there is a text that pits Spenta Mainyu against Angra Mainyu, be aware that it's a misinterpretation of key parts in the Gāthā (Gāt # 30, 45). The Gāthā talk about *two Mainyus* that are the wellspring of harmony or disharmony. No qualifying adjective is used in that section of the Gāthā. Also, if you ever see Ahura Mázdá pitted against Ahriman, you know the writer is influenced by the new Avesta. There's no Ahriman in the Gāthā.

14) The Gāthā are paradoxical in that the nature of their content may have contributed to their erosion and decline. How is that possible? <u>First</u>, the poems and chants are easy to transmit orally but hard to translate into prose in another language and still preserve the subtleties. As the archaic dialect of *Gāthāii* faded, so did the connection to the esoteric meaning. <u>Second</u>, Zártosht lived long ago in a remote area with little civilization. He did not have a successor to preserve and promote his teachings, or the backing of a power-seeking ruler to impose the teachings on the population and demand obedience. His message was categorically antithetical to such an attitude. By the time civilized society heard of Zártosht, only a name was left and his message had already been altered beyond recognition by the clergy group *moghs*. People had already been trained to bow their heads to authority and believed that the power of their ruler emanated from God's will and glory. <u>Third</u>, wisdom of the Gāthā is simple. Oh, but how difficult it is to seek that which is simple! It takes an introspective and mature culture to crave simple soul nourishment over that which sedates the masses and fattens religious and political bodies in power.

Flame is

    the inner-voice

        of a candle.

azarm

PART III

WISDOM SPEAKS

THE SECRET OF THE GOLDEN FLOWER

Those of you who are familiar with Jung's work may know that in 1928, the sinologist Richard Wilhelm, then director of the *China-Institut* in Frankfurt, gave Jung a copy of the Taoist alchemical treatise of the *Secret of the Golden Flower* that he had translated into German, inviting him to write a commentary. In a nutshell, this is a Chinese text on yoga and meditation as a way to access inner forces of the psyche. It's a practical guide for the integration of the personality. The text is rooted in a philosophy that we humans are microcosms, not separate from the macrocosm, and that *Tao*, or *the Way*, reveals laws of the universe that apply to both the visible and invisible realms.

Itself motionless, Tao is the means of all movement. Out of the Tao and the supreme ultimate develop the principles of reality and polarity—light (yang) and shade (yin) which can be expanded to encompass all polar opposites, including the sexual. In his discussion of the text and Chinese characters, Wilhelm mentions that the expression *Golden Flower*, in an esoteric and veiled way, contains the word *light*, and wonders about the origins of the light-religion. He mentions Zártosht, the many Persian temples in China from the T'ang period, and Persian mysticism but acknowledges that there are strong divergences. I suspect Wilhelm is correct in that the divergences he noted were due to the distortions that had already entered into Zártosht's teachings by then.

The individual who can penetrate the Center of the magic circle of polar duality returns to the undivided One, the Tao. So, while in Buddhism the goal is the complete deconstruction of the ego, like blowing out the flame of a candle, and returning to nirvana, in Taoism the goal is to preserve in a transformed way, the idea of the person, traces left by his experiences. He says the person is the light by means of which the life returns to itself and is symbolized in the Chinese text as the *Golden Flower*.

Jung was very touched by the ancient Chinese text and immediately saw it as a link between the insights of the East and his own independent psychological discoveries about the unconscious all the way across the globe. Nonetheless, he wisely cautioned the Westerner not to import eastern wisdom out of sheer imitation, consequently bypassing the task of making real his own deepest meaning. What Jung is saying is that medicine that heals one individual can be poison for another. In a way, Jung believed that Westerners ought to develop their own version of yoga. He was especially grateful that Wilhelm had recognized the wisdom in the ancient text and rescued it from metaphysics and offered it generously to the West. Unfortunately, Wilhelm died a few months after this offering and their collaboration ended.

After discovering the wisdom hidden in the Gāthā, I could identify with both Wilhelm and Jung. Like Wilhelm, I felt compelled to share my perception of Zártosht's universal message with others, especially at a point in our history when we're being torn apart by our appalling approach to polarity and differences. Like Jung, I saw numerous similarities between the wisdom of the Gāthā and Jung's discoveries about the psyche, only 3500 years apart.

Zártosht, like Siddhartha, Jesus, or Jung is an epochal man in that his ideas, way ahead of his time, usher in a whole new perspective, a new way of thinking that lays a foundation for the unification of the world through the alchemical transformation of one individual at a time. It is astonishing how relevant his ancient words are for us today though they were spoken 3500–3700 years ago.

An analogy might help convey my point. Suppose there is a necklace that has a few real pearls but the rest of its beads are costume jewelry. The Gāthā are like the genuine pearls, and the rest of the beads are the additions and misrepresentations that have happened over the years but sold as the real thing. This fact is known by many careful students of Mázdáism and is not what compels me to write this book.

Rather, I am going beyond this observation. *I am saying that even writers who recognize that the Gāthā are the genuine pearls, still show the fatal tendency to perceive this ancient text through the lens of religion and as a struggle between Good and Evil or worse, as abstract legalism.* These beliefs devalue the ancient text and tarnish the pearls. Surely, subliminal religious consciousness is quite different than the loaded word *Religion* we use today when translating the teachings of the Gāthā. For me, the Gāthā represent a way of Liberation from such shackles. By definition, a *way of Liberation* can't be pinned to a specific definition. We end up saying what it is not, like a sculptor removes the excess pieces of rocks from a block until an image appears.

I've looked at several translations of the Gāthā and paid attention to whether the translators show sensitivity to the translation pitfalls mentioned earlier. Many translations and interpretations left me cold because the author had viewed the Gāthā as a doctrine, a philosophy or an ideological religion. These are examples of pigeonholing that have saddled and damaged this ancient text. I feel let down when I see Zártosht, this ancient poetic sage, reduced to a bearded man on the cover of a book, or his teachings confused with worshiping fire by a priest in a fire temple. When we go through some of the key terms of the Gāthā, I hope you'll see what why the discrepancy in views is so disappointing.

I must emphasize that I am not claiming that my understanding of the Gāthā is *the* correct one, but I can assure you that I have viewed the text through several lenses and passed them through careful scrutiny. These lenses are different from those of a linguist, historian, or a passionate Mázdean believer. After reading a verse, if I couldn't find a confirmation in the sensible world (in fields such as physics, chemistry, anatomy, etc.) for what Zártosht had just said—*plus* a confirmation in all that I had learned about the unconscious through readings, dreams, and work with my patients, *plus* in my own life experiences as a woman—then I couldn't fully embrace that particular statement of the Gāthā. Like rethreading the three strands of mother's pearl necklace in the dream, every statement of the Gāthā has been submitted to a careful consideration by me, a scientist, depth psychologist, and woman, intertwined throughout the entire reading process ready to receive a unified strand that was emerging.

<u>Only when the essence of the Gāthā was freed from the shackles of concrete religion, mythology, metaphysics, and cultural bias did the ancient pearl show its timeless face to me.</u>

GĀTHĀII— A NEW, ANCIENT WORD

The more I heard the heartbeat of the Gātha, the more I wanted to stop using words such as Religion, Mázdean, Zoroastrian, Avesta, all of which are saddled with centuries of misrepresentation. I accept that as human psyche evolves, myths, beliefs, and language change over time. My objection arises when we use a key word today thinking that we are referring to *something* that has nothing, nothing to do anymore with the original meaning of that *something*. If I want to share the essence of Gātha with you, I'll be obliged to continually preface the conversation by saying, "Wait...no, it isn't what you thought it was." That's when language fails in its role as a bridge and becomes a cumbersome barrier. We need a remedy.

Language like a necklace is a string of words that have become habits of cultural convention. I propose to revive the word **Gāthāii** to help represent *my* understanding of the meaning of the Gātha and their life intuition once freed from religion, mythology, metaphysics, as well as cultural bias. I am intentionally leaving out many of the Avesta words that make the text more abstract and inaccessible. I'm only including the terms that I think are essential for you to grasp the meaning. What follows is a condensed summary and a discussion of the relevance of the Gātha to our lives. The insights are so modern that it is hard to believe a human being had such a poetic intuition of life 3500–3700 years ago. As I mentioned, it is also astonishingly simple. Maybe I should say it *appears* simple because the teachings present a process that still involves many internal phases of transformation and unfolding before an individual returns to the Origin.

You may recall that earlier I invited you to be patient with me as I paint a mural with a nail polish brush to introduce an *idea* for which the Western dualistic mind, as intelligent as it is, doesn't have a consciousness. That's coming up in the next section.

An architect who designs a multi-story building or a tailor who sews an outfit must have some image or idea in mind of what will eventually get formed and become a visible hotel or a tangible wedding dress. They need a pattern of some sort. In the same way, broadly speaking, different world cultures have three types of cosmologies that represent how our world came to be. The <u>first</u> is the Carpentry model (e.g. *Ideological* Abrahamic religions) in which God, like a carpenter, created the world one step at a time. The <u>second</u> is the Hindu notion of reality that resembles the game of God playing hide and seek; everything appears and disappears. Brahma creates the world in an act of self-forgetting or dismemberment, whereby the One becomes Many. He comes again to himself only to begin the play again. The <u>third</u> model views the world as an interconnected organism as a whole that is continuously growing and evolving. It's a mentality that makes, or forces, nothing but *grows* everything.

In my opinion, the *Gāthāii* Way fits the third model; similar pattern as seen in modern fields of Quantum physics, Genetics, Psychoneuroimmunology, etc.

A COMMENTARY ON THE GĀTHĀII INTUITION OF LIFE

In the *Gāthāii* Way, the undivided, nondual, germinal Center is called **Mázdá**. From this Center arise a pair of twin essences (two *Mainyus*), twin spirits, two forces that upon encountering each other, produce poles of "Life and *Un*life" (not the same as death). The two poles don't combat each other; they complete and complement one other. You may be more familiar with these poles as Yang and Yin, respectively.

As each pole struggles to complete itself and find its complementary half, a polarity is generated that's similar to the potential difference leading to flow of charge in an electric current. The positive and negative poles don't imply Good or Bad in a moral sense; they represent how we've agreed to show the direction of the flow. In the *Gāthāii* view, the polarity or flow of psychic energy is between these two poles.

- **Life** pole: a spectrum encompassing consciousness, creative element, spiritual, Light, ideal, eternal, action, heat, stimulation, discipline and separateness, differentiation, individualization, penetrating, movement associated with strength, meaning, will.

and

- **Unlife** pole: a spectrum representing quiescence, nature, stillness receptive element, instinctual, unconscious, yielding, wet, shade, non-spiritual, non-ideal, perishable, undifferentiated and collective, inert, gestating, lifegiving and devouring.

The unfolding of *all* polarities follows a rhythm, a pattern, a universal and an unalterable Law known as **Áshá**. We first recognize these polarities existing *outside* of ourselves as Laws of the Universe governing the movement of planets and changes of seasons, rain and drought, light and shade, egg hatching, flesh decaying, but the same laws and polarities apply just as much to us humans.

It's more difficult for us to notice the polarities that exist within us, for as soon as we do, we tend to quickly break the tension (split it) and favor one pole over the other. (The pole we reject in ourselves becomes the enemy!)

Holding the tension of polarity between Life/Unlife without splitting demands the same attention as walking a tightrope. It's akin to smelling without inhaling, seeing without squinting, holding without holding on, touching without grabbing. There is no right or wrong, good or bad associated with these happenings. They are processes that are mutually aris*ing*, becom*ing*, expand*ing*, contract*ing*, grow*ing*, decay*ing*, at once, unanimously, spontaneously throbb*ing* like a pulse in a giant organism.

The <u>Gāthāii</u> view is an expression of a mentality that feels completely at home in this universe. Human being is an integral part of his environment. Nature is as much our mother as our father. It's a vision of a world whose fundamental principle is relativity rather than warfare.

Good and Evil do not have an existence in the world independent of the human being. Volcanoes, earthquakes, lions killing gazelles are not evil. It's an individual's choices that become the source of what eventually unfolds in the scene of the world as Good or Evil. Hitler and Stalin were not natural disasters. They were individuals who fomented a collective madness that unleashed murder, genocide, and devastation on the world. Such events are not *natural* but are rather the product of human willfulness gone to extremes in ways that can only be called *evil*.

We experience the consequences of our Thoughts/Words/Actions *internally* as a hell or heaven—states we have created within ourselves. And sometimes we live out our inward hell in our personal and political relationships, thus casting one another into a hell of our own making.

From *Gāthāii* perspective, an individual is not born a sinner. There is trust in the essential goodness of human nature, for every human being still contains a scintilla of a vital energy from the germinal Center that's left in him. Every human is entrusted, even if in embryonic form, with the freedom to reflect and consult his conscience before choosing his words and actions.

Our ability to discern and make this choice depends on our knowledge (conscious thought, reason) *and* inner wisdom (intuition). The Wise choose Thoughts/Words/Actions which are (*Vohu*)—in harmony with this unalterable rhythm. The Unwise choose Thoughts/Words/Actions which are (*Akem*)—disharmonious to the universal Law of Universe.

At the beginning of the book, I asked "In what mode does the inner voice communicate with us?" How do we know how to cultivate thoughts that are in harmony with the rhythm of life? What generates Wisdom, or what Buddhism calls "the Wise Mind," Christianity "The mind of Christ," and Judaism "the Shekhinah of the soul"? What is the difference between Wisdom and an ordinary thought?

In the Gāthā the mental function that works through all this knowing and discerning is designated with the word **Vohu Mana**, which has been often translated as Perfect Thought or Pure Mind. My concern with such translations is that they reduce *Vohu Mana* to yet another moral judgment. This word *Vohu Mana* is so important in understanding the Gāthāii view that we need to try to intuit the original dwelling place of such a *Thought*.

Just as we associate the womb as the organ within which a fetus grows, or the ears as organs responsible for hearing and balance, I lean toward translating **Vohu Mana** as the <u>organ of wisdom</u>. Where is this organ? Is there a *place* in our body where this special kind of thinking takes place?

The Center for this activity is neither what we associate with the ego nor the Heart. Mind is too cerebral and the notion of Heart is too emotional—almost sentimental. The difficulty is the *organ* that allows us to have thoughts has no thought itself! Like the eye that functions well allows us to see but doesn't see itself, or like fire that doesn't burn itself.

Wisdom includes both conscious thinking *and* intuition. It isn't just good thinking. So, the *organ of wisdom* is the Center where thinking and intuition unite. You may remember from earlier discussion that the Farsi word for Thought (*ándisheh*) comes from the ancient Iranian language of Avesta and means *apparition of a body or a figure*—same as Jung's notion of *personifying*. We can't will or force this process. It happens spontaneously. It emphatically is not the same as imagination or guided imagery. (At this moment I am painting a mural with a nail polish brush. We'll go slowly because I'm trying to introduce something that our Western mind isn't used to.)

Suppose there is a mirror in your hallway. If you slowly slide sideways toward the mirror, there comes a moment when your entire figure shows up in the mirror and your eyes meet the eyes of the image looking back at you. It's at that moment that you see your image. The mirror just happens to be the privileged surface where this encounter take place. The reflection could have taken place on the surface of water in a pond.

Meditation on this *organ of wisdom* does not evoke the same process as thinking about the weather or deciding what to fix for dinner. It does not generate a *fantasy* either. It's not visualizing an object like a banana that you've already seen somewhere. What does it evoke?

When we meditate on this *organ of wisdom* and turn the gaze inward as if we're approaching an inner mirror, the *outline of a figure*, an Image, that exists *a priori* in the psyche *appears—That is a Thought*. In *this* Thought, resides **Armáiti**, which is stillness, serenity. This is a T̲hought under the pure gaze of quiescence, T̲hought of quietude, gentleness, silent meditation, patience, serenity. This T̲hought is W̲isdom. (I underline the T in T̲hought to distinguish it from all the other thoughts we have.)

Now, if I learn to stop tinkering and leave this *organ* alone to function in a naturally spontaneous way, this organ will be the wellspring of a T̲hought within which resides a W̲ord and an A̲ction so that, when allowed to unfold in unison, they flow together in harmony with the rhythm and laws of the universe—with **Áshá**.

Such T̲houghts contain a certain creative power or virtue that should not be equated with moral rectitude. This power has effectiveness in the same way that a spice or medicinal herb has healing power. This power is called **Khshathra**, which has been translated as Spiritual Power or energy, desirable reign and sovereignty. I translate it as <u>empowering energy</u>. Think of it as an activating energy that you need to both keep inwardly (stillness) *and* release outwardly (action). It's like the energy of water. If it is held in reservoir and never released; it won't generate electricity. On the other hand, if we let it dissipate into the ground, there won't be any potential energy to harness later. The two streams of energy are similar to Jung's concepts of Introversion and Extraversion, except that Jung's concepts apply to psychic energy only, whereas the Gāthāii concept encompasses both psychic and physiological processes.

Khshathra then is the energy or power that flows inwardly to intensify and become effective willpower, and that flows outwardly as <u>A</u>ction in harmony with the unalterable rhythm of the universe. There is an alchemical transmutation and development that happens in an individual at this stage in that he becomes aware of something larger than himself. This awareness relativizes him and leads to reining in his unchecked greed and self-centeredness. It calls for inner-sovereignty and a grounding of the will.

Unfortunately, The term *Khshathra*, self-sovereignty, was later abused and linked to the sovereignty of a king (shah) over his people, thus gradually paving the way for subservience, just as people also sometimes submit to the will of an objectified God without questioning it.

From the *Gāthāii* perspective, the Trilogy of <u>T</u>hought/<u>W</u>ord/<u>A</u>ction is so interconnected that it becomes a spontaneous glimpse into a person's true nature. I cannot conceal forever who I am. I become my thoughts, words, and action. To the extent that I meditate on the *organ of wisdom*, I give birth to <u>T</u>houghts, <u>W</u>ords and <u>A</u>ctions in harmony with rhythm of the universe, and substantiate, bring to life a more whole *me*, who is in service of others for the renewal of the world. This is <u>Wholeness and Integration</u> (**Haurvatāt**).

That which I think, say and do to myself and unto others leaves a trace in nature and the world, which lasts beyond time. This represents the notion of <u>Timelessness</u> (**Amertat**) in the *Gāthāii* way.

The destiny of the world is entrusted to the transmutative power within each one of us and the extent to which we embody the six attributes. Such is the profound meaning of the Gāthā verse:

> **"May we be among those who bring about the transformation of the world." (Gāt #30, 9)**

It's not enough to cultivate wise Thoughts and Actions. I must also consider my own wellbeing. Yet, I mustn't withdraw from the world like a hermit or sit passively for others to carry my load in life. I must also be aware of my impact on my surrounding and those around me and consciously help others cultivate their best. You and I may have different thoughts and maybe even opposing points of view. That's why we also need words to share our ideas with each other—and then—listen to one another. The Farsi (not Arabic) word for arguing is *Āruzidan*, which comes from the Avesta root *āroc* meaning to *enlighten*. Words that enlighten....

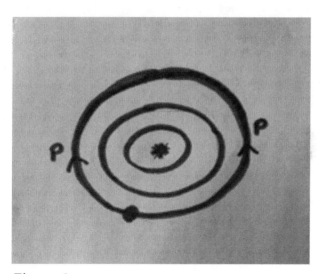

Figure 1

In the <u>Gāthāii</u> way, there is a mutually dependent relationship between me (the solid dot on the circle) and that ineffable, germinal Center ✶, **Mázdá**, or (*It*), out of which I grew. The points labeled "P" represent polarities. *I* and *It* are interdependent, connected. There is no *I* without *It*; there is no *It* to know without an *I* to see.

I am a cloud...

always looking for my Mother

I ask the birds about her whereabouts

I follow the wind hoping It'll take me to her

For a moment I stand still over the sea
In the mirror of water, I stare at her face

I can no longer tell...
Did she birth me? Did I birth her?

azarm

What I just discussed—*Vohu Mana, Áshá, Khshathra, Armáiti, Haurvatāt, Amertat*) are six aspects of the germinal Center that like the radius of a circle connect me directly to the Center. These are powers or attributes that I and the germinal Center* mutually share. I want to draw your attention to the perfect balance and tension that exists between the six powers in that three of the attributes (*Vohu Mana, Áshá, Khshathra*) represent the pole of <u>Life</u> (thought, rhythm/order, action), while the other three (*Armáiti, Haurvatāt, Amertat*) represent the pole of <u>Unlife</u> (quiescence, wholeness, immortality).

Remember Dream #2 that I shared earlier (on page 53), in which I was walking down the aisle as a bride holding a clay figurine? I said I eventually learned that the figurine represented Armáiti. Now we can appreciate the profound message of the dream showing me (bride) a path toward a marriage of Quiescence (figurine) with <u>T</u>hought (creative spirit) to produce Wisdom. In a way, this was a dream for all of us, not just me.

The measure of my wholeness will be the degree to which I have the consciousness to carry these attributes within me. To the extent that I meditate, cultivate, activate and intensify these six powers within me, and in the world around me, the alchemical transmutation continues. The circle in the diagram gets smaller, smaller, and smaller, polarities within me diminish (the two P's in the diagram), and I become more whole as I approach the Center. In other words, "*I*" am no other than the totality of things of which I am aware.

There is a beautiful paragraph (#512) in Jung's final life work, *Mysterium Coniunctionis*, that describes the standards of thought and action necessary if we are to carry the opposites within us and reconcile the polarities.

Jung says:

> "If the projected conflict is to be healed, it must return to the psyche of the individual, where it had its unconscious beginnings. He must celebrate a last supper with himself, and eat his own flesh, and drink his own blood, which means that he must recognize and accept the other in himself.... Is this perhaps the meaning of Christ's teaching, that each must bear his own cross? For if you have to endure yourself, how would you be able to rend others also?"

Earlier, I mentioned the poet Hāfez who uses the image of the geometric compass used for drawing arcs and circles, and says:

"Like a compass I wander in smaller and smaller circles, never reaching the Center."

Only in that Center are all polarities unified and reconciled in the psyche. It is a return to the nondual One. Death is the goal of a Conscious life when polarities of *Life* and *Unlife* unite. This is the <u>Gāthāii</u> vision of the process Jung called Individuation.

Jung ends his controversial work, *Answer to Job*, with a paragraph that is an identical twin to what I just presented as my perception of the relationship between an individual and the Center in the <u>Gāthāii</u> way (Figure 1). By *Christification,* he means the time has come for each of us, one person at a time, to work toward embodying Christ attributes that pull us closer to the Center.

Jung says:

"... There then arises that reciprocal action between two autonomous factors which compels us, when describing and explaining processes, to present sometimes the one and sometimes the other factor as the acting subject, even when God becomes man. The Christian solution has hitherto avoided this difficulty by recognizing Christ as the one and only God-man. But the indwelling of the Holy Ghost, the third Divine Person, in man, brings about the *Christification* of many..." [*italics* added].

Another way of being with this is to start from the Center and to keep widening the circles. Like a seed or an embryo that grows to become a plant, animal or a human, this Center is a densely packed core that, though it appears invisible to us, contains the pattern and everything it needs. Surely, you have seen blades of propellers in aircrafts rotating so fast in the air that you don't see the blades and think there is nothing there. You'd know they are there if you dared to stick your finger in them! As the propellers slow down, they become more visible and eventually we can even count their blades.

Though itself invisible, as this core of energy (pure Consciousness?) expands, takes Form (incarnates), it becomes visible to us as tree, hummingbird, baby, rocks, red blood cell, and a million other Forms. Another Persian poet (Hātef) says,

"*from colorless water, a thousand colors*"

No verb. No need for a verb. You see how this is an example of a metaphor in a nondual language that creates no splitting? Rilke has a beautiful poem that speaks to this. ***"I live my life in widening circles."*** With his last line he says, ***"Am I a falcon, a storm, or a great song?"***

It was an ordinary day. I had boiled chicken thighs and poured the broth in a glass bowl on the counter to cool before I put it in the fridge. Small oil droplets were rising to the surface; I continued doing chores and touched the bowl now and then to see if it's cool enough to put in the fridge. Then, something stopped me.

I saw a pattern beginning to form on the surface of the broth. Something pulled me deep into what was being formed as it was being formed... my heart started beating faster. I felt a rush in me and around me...like an energy but nothing was moving in the kitchen; soon small and bigger rings covered the entire surface of the bowl. Every ring had six sides. What was it that flowed through the broth to make it become that shape? Was it the same as what I felt in my body? I looked at the persimmons and pears in the fruit bowl, the rosemary bush outside, my dog napping calmly in her bed, and saw the same creative energy that had flowed through all of them, informing them to become different figures and bodies, now appearing as a persimmon, a rosemary bush, or my dog.

Can't name (It) ...can't not name (It)

Can't hear (It)...can't not hear (It) as inner voice

    (It) Plums the tree

        Whirlpools the river

        Moves the wind

        Wails the flute

        Burns the fire

        Wets the tear

            Beats my heart—

            Breaks my heart

                azarm

GLOSSARY

Akem A word mentioned in the Gāthā. Though it has been mistranslated as Bad and Deceitful, Akem is the choice the unwise makes that is *not* aligned with the rhythm or with the universal Laws of Universe.

Alchemy Alchemy looks at the unconscious and the process of transformation of the personality from a symbolic perspective. Medieval alchemists, forerunners of modern chemists, sought to turn base metals into gold. Jung found in their work a profound symbolism of the processes of individuation.

Amertat A word mentioned in the Gāthā. It is one of the six attributes of Mázdá and represents Timelessness.

Amesha Spenta This is not mentioned in the Gāthā, not even once. The six *aspects* of Mázdá presented in the Gāthā appear in the (adulterated) Avesta as six Archangels and are presented as separate entities called *amesha spenta* (Holy Immortals) in the new Avesta. The six aspects are indeed mentioned in the Gāthā but never as a group, nor anthropomorphized as separate figures the way they are in the new (adulterated) Avesta.

Angra A word in the Gāthā. A spirit that is disharmonious with rhythm of Life and Laws of the Universe. Represents the complementary pole of Spenta. See *Spenta*.

Anima According to Jung, ani*ma* represents the archetype of a man's *yin*, just an anim*us* represents the archetype of a woman's *yang*. Even though every man carries a recessed feminine in him, the field of expression of this archetype is often obscure and fear inspiring. This archetype is contrasexual and shows that nothing is so totally other than the opposite sex. A man doing deeply integrative work must be disciplined in treating his anima with respect, allowing her to come into expression so that he can learn from her.

Armáiti   (*Armá-y-ti*) One of the six attributes of Mázdá mentioned in the Gāthā. It represents quiescence, serenity, patience. If translated into Jungian terms, it would be the anima or the archetype of the Eternal Feminine.

Áshá   An important word mentioned in the Gāthā; represents the suchness of nature—that which goes with the Rhythm of life and the universal and unalterable Laws of the Universe. Áshá it is one of the six attributes of Mázdá and is the Vedic equivalent of Rita.

Avesta   This word can either refer to a book or to an ancient language.

a) As a <u>book</u>, it is the collection of sacred Mázdean teachings, many of which were written long after Zártosht. Today's Avesta book is a collection of five parts (Yasna, Visparad, Vendidad, Yasht, and Khordeh or little Avesta). Each part is briefly explained in this Glossary. The only part of Avesta that came directly from Zártosht himself is the Gāthā.

b) As a <u>language</u>, Avesta is one of the ancient Iranian languages that belonged to the eastern part of Iran. Avesta is older than Sanskrit by a few centuries. The alphabet has 48 characters and can be expanded to a more detailed form of 53 (37 consonants and 16 vowels). It's written from right to left and a dot is placed after each word. Avesta has one of the most precise alphabets in the world. The picture on page 92 shows what Avesta alphabet looks like as seen in the Gāthā. (See Poordavood in the Sources Consulted).

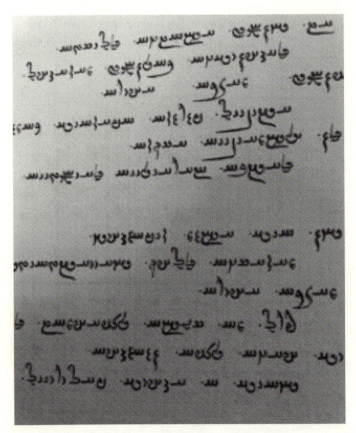

Avesta alphabet, as seen in the Gāthā.

Depth Psychology This term is used today in its original sense to identify and describe those who study and are concerned with the phenomenon of the unconscious.

Extraversion A term from Jung's Typology that refers to a basic attitude toward the world in which an individual is more energized by the external world. Jung was interested in how *consciousness* works in different ways in different people. The extravert orients himself predominantly by the collective norms and the spirit of his times.

Gaethya A word mentioned in the Gāthā. It has been related to the earth and the Material. I see it as related to terrestrial and the sensible realm; that which has *Form*. Gaethya is the counter pole to Mainyu.

Gāthā The only part of the Avesta Book that came directly from Zártosht himself are the Gāthā. These are chants and poems and they represent an intimate dialogue between Zártosht and Mázdá. The Gāthā are dispersed throughout the Yasna section of the book of Avesta.

Gāthāii (or Gathic) is the dialect in which the Gāthā were uttered. This dialect fell into oblivion. The word *Gāthāii* is used by the author to represent a new way of viewing the Gāthā after they've been liberated from metaphysics, religion, mythology and other misperceptions.

Hāfez Persian lyric poet (d. 1390) famous for his ghazals that are usually 7-11 couplets, steeped in layers of metaphor and mystery. Hāfez is a common last name. This poet is known as Hāfez-e-Shiraz, in reference to the city of Shiraz where he was born and is buried.

Hatef Persian poet (d.1783) mostly known for his elegy called Realm of Love (*Eghleemé Eshgh*).

Haurvatāt A word from the Gāthā. It is one of the six attributes of Mázdá. Represents Wholeness, similar to Jung's concept of Individuation.

Individuation A key concept in Jung's contribution to how a personality develops. As a person becomes himself, whole and distinct from the collective, he becomes conscious of the ways he is unique and, at the same time, like every other person. The individuation process, when not inhibited or distorted, is the psychic parallel to the physical process of growth and aging. "The aim of Individuation is nothing less than to divest the self of the false wrappings of the persona on the one hand, and the suggestive power of the primordial images on the other" (CW 7, Para 269).

Introversion A term from Jung's Typology that refers to a basic attitude toward the world in which an individual is more energized by the internal world. The object plays at most a secondary role. The introvert's move in every situation that faces him is to recoil. As a person matures, Jung speculated that various typological opposites merge to bring a richer personality.

Jung, C.G. Carl Gustave Jung (d. 1961) was a Swiss psychiatrist and psychoanalyst who founded the idea of Analytical Psychology. Prolific writer, he is one of the most influential figures of 20th century and pioneers in the field of psychology. His well-known autobiography is called *Memories, Dreams and Reflections*.

Khordeh Avesta Or Little Avesta is a book of common prayers, part of which are in a modern version of Farsi. Khordeh Avesta is now one of the sections in the book of Avesta. The contents do not come from Zártosht's teachings.

Khshathra A word from the Gāthā that represents one of the six attributes of Mázdá. I translate it as <u>empowering energy</u>, self-sovereignty, desirable reign. It is an activating energy that one needs to both keep inwardly (stillness, willpower) *and* release outwardly (action).

Magavan A word mentioned in the Gāthā. *Maga* in Sanskrit means reward, wealth, blessing. Magavan in the Gāthā is similar to the Sanskrit word and means the *one who possesses Maga*. In the context of the Gāthā, it refers to a supportive group of Zártosht's followers. Unlike what some translators have assumed, Magavan that appears in the

Gatha should not be translated as mogh—the group that later distorted the Gāthā.

Mainyu A word mentioned in the Gāthā. It is derived from the infinitive *man*, meaning to think or meditate. It refers to that which is invisible, mental and spiritual. It's the counter pole to Gaethya.

Mandala (Pronounced mánn-dálá) Means *magic circle* in Sanskrit. It's a geometric figure with a circle within a square or a square encircled. Jung interpreted it as an expression of the Self. A mandala can appear in a dream and represent potential for wholeness; it can also help bind a person's sense of fragmentation during distressful and chaotic times.

Manichaeism A religion founded by Mani in Persia in the 3rd century AD. Manichaeism held that the world was a fusion of spirit and matter, the original principles of good and evil, and that the fallen soul was trapped in the evil, material world and could reach the transcendent world only by way of the spirit.

Mani lurks in the Western psyche through Augustine, who was a Manichaean until he converted to Christianity. From then on, Augustine did a great deal to identify Mani with the devil. Mani's doctrine was a concoction influenced by Buddhism, Christianity, and Zoroastrianism.

Mani's doctrine was the opposite of Augustine's Christian idea of *Privatio Boni* (Evil is the absence of good. It doesn't exist as a substantial entity.) Mani, on the other hand, asserted that evil had the same reality and was made of the same substance as was good.

The Manichaean doctrine was spread through the Roman empire and the East by missionaries. It disappeared almost entirely from Western Europe by the end of the 5th century but survived in Asia until the 14th century.

Mázdá The unknowable inner Center that has been given names such as *Tao, Atman, It, Tathata, Self*, was called by Zártosht as *Mázdá*.

Mázdá means Big Mind, Source of Wisdom. It also means Grower of Life.

Mázdáism An interchangeable term with Zoroastrianism. Refers to those who believe they are following the teachings of Zártosht.

Medes An Iranian tribe. The Medes are ethnically today's Kurds. They formed the first Iranian empire by defeating the Assyrians in 612 BC. Together with the help of Persians and help of Cyrus II the Great, they formed the Achaemenian Empire in 538 BC. This dynasty came to an end when the last king, Darius III, was defeated by Alexander the Great in 334 BC.

Mithraism Mithra was an important deity to Indo-Iranians before Zártosht and became important again in the new Avesta, even though Zártosht had strongly rejected the worship of many Aryan gods and anthropomorphism in general. *Moghs* were responsible for reintroducing the pre-Zártosht Aryan practices of Mithraism into what they presented as Mázdean teachings.

Mithra was an important deity to Aryan groups Romans, and Greeks and not just Indo-Iranians. Mithraism spread from India all the way to Europe. The cult first appeared in the late 1st century AD and, at an extraordinary pace, spread from the Italian Peninsula and border regions across the whole of the Roman empire. Until the accession of Constantine, Mithraism had all but appeared to become the religion of the entire Roman empire. Its influence on many Christian symbolism continues to be discussed (Mithra's birthday on December 25th, ringing of church bells, bishop's red cap, drinking of wine at Mass, etc.).

Mithra means contract, friendship, also light emanating from the sun (not the sun itself).

Mogh A powerful priestly clan at the time of Achaemenians and amongst the Medes in northwest of Iran. After several centuries when Zártosht's teachings had already deteriorated and had been altered by the clergy in the eastern part of Iran, the Moghs from the western part created a concoction, reintroduced many of their old Aryan practices that Zártosht had strongly rejected, and presented it as Zártosht's teachings.

Myth A myth is like a collective dream. It's important not to take a myth literally, although many do. Myths present a narrative that is trans-personal and which provides the essential container for psychic expression in an individual's life. Jung said that we don't invent myths; we experience them. Gods and goddesses in myths represent a basic pattern that unfolds in the stories of their descendants. Myths show what happens when an archetype has free rein in lives where there is no differentiation.

Personification The ability to *personify* underlies all psychic life. Personification is the psychological activity in which all that one experiences is spontaneously *personified*—related to as a *person*. We experience personification in dreams and fantasies. A person who cannot personify tends to personalize everything. In Jungian analysis, a person's relationship to his personifications are explored.

Psyche For Jung, psyche (or psychic) represents the totality of psychic processes of conscious and unconscious. His writings about the psyche suggest that it is a structure made for movement, growth, and transformation.

Rilke Rainer Maria Rilke (d.1926). Austro-German lyrical poet who became internationally known with such works as Duino Elegies and Sonnets to Orpheus.

Scheffler Johannes Scheffler (d.1967) was born into a noble Polish Lutheran family. He studied philosophy and later became a physician. Angelus Silesius is his monastic name. The writings of the German mystic Jacob Boehme influenced him but that didn't sit well with the Lutheranism of the time. He converted to Catholicism and took the name Angelus.

Self The term Self can be confusing because "self" in lower case refers to an individual, whereas when capitalized, Self refers to the totality of the psyche. When it appears at the beginning of a sentence, in order to avoid confusion, I have adopted the practice of underlining the S in Self when it refers to the totality of the psyche. Self is Jung's equivalent term for Atman, Tao, Mázdá.

Shadow Jung's succinct definition of shadow is, "The thing a person has no wish to be" (CW 16, para 470). Shadow is not necessarily what is dark—it's *what's in the dark* in the sense of being outside of the ego-ideal, and generally outside of conscious awareness. We all have a shadow. Given that shadow is an archetype, its contents are powerful and can overwhelm a person. In psychotherapy, the patient gradually becomes aware of the images and situations that lead to projecting the shadow on others.

Spenta A word mentioned in the Gāthā. It's an adjective and means Holy, bounteous, a Spirit that is continuously moving toward the harmony with the rhythm of life and the Laws of the Universe. Represents the complementary pole of Angra.

Symbol A Symbol is not an agreed upon sign like $ or % in mathematics. Symbols are metaphoric portrayal of psychic reality. According to Jung, a true symbol attempts to express something for which no verbal concept yet exists. The symbolic process is an experience in images and of images.

Its development is consistent with the principle that a given position eventually moves in the direction of its opposite. "... it thus forms the middle ground on which opposites can be united (CW 6, para 825).

Trilogy   A set of three that are interconnected, in unison. A triad, or trio, on the other hand, is a group or set of three people or things.

Unconscious   Like Freud, Jung used the term unconscious to refer to psychic contents that are not accessible to the waking ego. Unlike Freud, Jung did not consider the unconscious to be nothing more than a repository of only infantile and repressed Personal material. Jung went beyond Freud in amplifying the unconscious to include the phylogenetic, instinctual basis of the human race. The *personal unconscious* is part of the *collective unconscious* or what he later called the Objective Psyche. The collective unconscious is independent of the ego. The unconscious is amoral. Jung thought morality is left to the individual.

Vendidad   A part of the current Avesta. Vendidad did not come from Zártosht himself and was most likely compiled in the Parthian period (247 BC to 224 AD). It is mostly concerned with the purity law, hygiene, and fighting against evil forces. Its name is a corruption of the Avesta word *vidaevadata,* which means against the Daevas (evil beings).

Visparad   This is one of the sections of the current book of Avesta, <u>not</u> stated by Zártosht himself. Visparad means [worship of] *All the Masters.* This long liturgy is solemnized on the seven great holy days of the faith.

Vohu   A word mentioned in the Gāthā. Although it has been mistranslated as Righteous and Good, Vohu is fundamentally that which is aligned with the Way, in harmony with Laws of the Universe.

Vohu mana   A word mentioned in the Gāthā meaning Organ of Wisdom, Perfect Thought. It's one of the six attributes of Mázdá.

Yasht   A section of the current book of Avesta that has <u>not</u> come from Zártosht himself. It deals with daily rituals of worship of Yazatas (meaning adorable ones, *Izad* in Farsi). These divinities correspond to Devas of the Hindus.

Yasna   Yasna means veneration, praying, celebration. The Farsi word *jashn* (feast, celebration) comes from Yasn. Yasna is a part of the current book of Avesta and consists of prose and poems. The poem part is known as the Gāthā, which are dispersed throughout the Yasna. Yasna deals with purpose of life, law of consequences, immortality of soul, and renovation of the world.

Zártosht   Also known as Zarathustra or Zoroaster, he is estimated to have lived 3700-3500 years ago near the Aral lake in Central Asia. For millions, he is the initiator of the religion of Zoroastrianism or Mázdáism. The only part of the sacred texts of Mázdáism that originate by Zártosht himself are the chants known as the Gāthā.

Zoroastrianism   (see Mázdáism)

Zurvanism   Contrary to popular belief, Zurvanism has nothing to do with Mázdáism. Like many pre-Zártosht Aryan practices, Zurvanism was brought back by the clergy group Moghs and presented as Zártosht's teachings.

Background: Some say that Zurvan was an old Aryan god of time (like Cronos, the old Greek god of Time). Others say that the first mention of a god of time amongst Iranians occurs several centuries after Zártosht's. Zurvan or eternal time was one of the new Avesta's minor gods. During the Sassanid dynasty (224 to 651 AD), and influenced by

Manichaeism, Zurvan became the supreme deity. Zurvanism was a mythology advanced by Moslems to deal with the unacceptable (perceived) dualistic religion of Zoroastrianism. Zurvan became <u>one</u> God and the father of two sons: Ahriman (Satan) and Ohrmazd (good god).

IN CASE YOU HAVE WONDERED

Is the Farsi alphabet the same as Arabic?

<u>Short answer</u>: It is the same now but it hasn't always been. Iranians today speak Farsi Dári but write it with an alphabet that they had helped create for the Arabic language.

<u>Longer answer</u>: At the time of the Arab Conquest (630+ AD), the language of Iranians was Pahlavi (see Table 1, page 47). Earlier I mentioned that while Iranians lost their Pahlavi language, another Iranian language (Farsi Dári) from the east of Iran gradually replaced it. At the beginning, Farsi Dári didn't have its own alphabet and was written in Pahlavi, Hebrew, or Soghdi alphabets.

Invading Arabs had not seen books and didn't have an alphabet. They had no currency for exchange either. Their Koran had been passed on orally but had not yet been recorded in writing. Iranians played an important role in creating the current Arabic alphabet and its grammar, but this alphabet is not well-suited for the Farsi language. Farsi is an Indo-European language, while Arabic is Semitic. The alphabet created for the Arabic language doesn't have letters for vowels (like o, a, é) that Farsi needs. Unless a mark like an accent is placed above or below a consonant (e.g., L), the reader can't tell whether that letter L within a word should be pronounced Lo, La, or Lé. This creates great ambiguity when reading unfamiliar Farsi words. Furthermore, because Farsi needs four additional sounds not heard in the Arabic language, Farsi added (P, Jé, gu, ch) to the alphabet they created.

We don't know exactly when the alphabet created for Arabic started being used for Farsi Dári. Some say 12th century AD. (There's evidence to show that the Pahlavi language was still being used in isolated parts of Iran as late as the 10th century AD.). The point to note is that the change of alphabet, for speakers of Farsi, from Pahlavi alphabet to Arabic, happened much later than the forced conversion to Islam and the loss of the Pahlavi language. (See Khanlari in Sources Consulted.)

Is Persian the same as Iranian?

<u>Short answer</u>: Practically speaking, yes.

<u>Longer answer</u>: Iranians living in Iran don't call themselves Persian. Abroad, and especially since the establishment of the Islamic Republic of Iran (1979), some Iranians refer to themselves as Persians to distance themselves from the negative connotations associated with the Islamic Republic currently in power in Iran. Thus, "Iran" is used in the context of political discussions, while both "Iran" and "Persia" are used when the discussion refers more to the cultural context

It helps to know whether we're referring to a nation's geographical area (territory that can expand and shrink due to wars) or to the cultural and linguistic lineages that connect a group of people. Today's Iran consists of a large number of different ethnic and tribal groups. People who identify themselves as Persian make up the majority, but there are large numbers of Guiláki, Āzári, and Kurdish people, as well. They are all citizens of Iran.

Is Mázdáism interchangeable with Zoroastrianism?

Yes. Zoroastrianism points the discussion toward Zártosht the founder, whereas Mázdáism directs it toward Mázdá, the nondual Center. Following are a few other synonyms.

<u>Parsees</u>: Persian Mázdeans who were persecuted in Iran following the Arab Conquest fled to India and are known as Parsees. They practice an orthodox version of the teachings.

<u>Beh-din</u>: Amongst themselves, Mázdeans refer to each other as Beh-din, which means Good Religion.

<u>Mázdáyasnan</u>: This is a generic term that means followers of Mázdáism.

Is the Gāthāii view of an individual's transformation in life similar to Alchemical transmutation?
Short answer: Yes. Except the Gāthā are expressed as poems/chants and not in abstruse language.

Longer answer: The aim of alchemists was simple, but their language and symbolism were complex. Basically, they wanted to create a miraculous substance (Philosophers' stone). Their method was to find suitable material (Prima Materia) and subject it to a series of operations that would turn it into the Philosophers' stone. Alchemical texts, though mysterious and even chaotic, show us the transformation that takes place in the personality on the journey toward wholeness. We see some of the same images in our dreams today.

Jung saw that it fell on alchemy to pick up the problem that his Swiss Reformation form of Christianity had left unaddressed. Ideological Christian psychology promotes the *suppression* of evil, whereas alchemy attempted a certain *transformation* of evil with a view to its future integration. Jung found in alchemy new possibilities for a deeper and more mystical Christian psychology. The final step in the alchemical procedure when the opposites are united is called the *coniunctio*. The Gāthāii lens acknowledges the reality of the polarity and shows us a path for transformation toward wholeness. To the extent that we humans cultivate the six attributes of Mázdá within ourselves, we move toward the integration of the opposites within us.

If I want to learn more about the Gāthā, what can I read?
I have not come across an English or Farsi interpretation of the Gāthā that satisfies all sides of my mind. Therefore, I cannot suggest a specific resource. Throughout the book, I have presented my reservations and concerns about the currently available interpretations of the Gāthā. Many of those who speak from within the tradition interpret the

Gāthā with warmth and passion but can't seem to free themselves from the dualistic, post-Islamic lens, or from using Arabic-derived words in the process of translations from Avesta to Farsi. Those who attempt to be more objective by presenting a cultural, historical and linguistic background end up dropping the Western reader in a sea of foreign words assuming he'll swim his way to the shore.

<u>Resources in English</u>: My suggestion is to come in through the back door. Any concise but comprehensive introduction to Jung or Taoism would be a good start. Jung's work becomes more complex and difficult to understand in the latter half of his life, but at the same time his insights increasingly converge with the life intuition of the Gāthā.

Here's what I mean. The subtitle to Jung's final work, *Mysterium Coniunctionis*, is "An Inquiry into the Separation and Synthesis of Opposites in Alchemy." It's a monumental study. You don't have to start there. You can slowly approach his extraordinarily fertile work by reading Jung's memoir, or books by Jacobi, Whitmont, or any of Edinger's fine works (see Sources Consulted), and branch out from there. Edinger is especially known for elucidating Jung's work on alchemy and Christianity.

If you want to enter from the front door, Mills, Taraporewala, Mehr and Khazai are listed in Sources Consulted. Their works include discussion of Mázdáism plus translation of the hymns in English. Mills provides a comprehensive analysis and interpretation of the Gāthā. Khazai's is a very short and introductory book. Mehr's book does not contain a translation of the Gāthā; he outlines the spirituality and principles of Zoroastrianism. Taraporewala's book contains helpful comments and historical perspective, but he, too, is influenced by the new Avesta. He does not conceal the fact that he is a devout Mázdean.

Resources in Farsi: The translations by Āzárgoshasb and Poordavood are done with scholarly intent (see Sources Consulted). Āzárgoshasb (1972) translates the Gāthā from Avesta and includes extensive interpretation and comparison with works of other scholars. He avoids using many Avesta words in his free-flowing translation. This approach has the benefit of keeping the Farsi more accessible for contemporary Iranians but leaves the door open to learning an ancient Avesta word through a post-Islamic lens. His (1981) work is a highly condensed version of the author's 1972 work. Poordavood's perspective at times shows influences from life in India and Vedic texts.

Was Hāfez a Mázdean?
Hāfez escapes all pigeonholing attempts, but this doesn't stop various factions from wanting to claim him as one of their own. He is a mirror in which the reader sees a reflection of his own inner world and thus many conclude that that's what Hāfez is all about.

Many have attempted to translate Hāfez's poems into poetry in other languages, similar to what Fitzgerald's translations created with Omar Khayyam's Robaiyat. This is a noble aspiration, but I think it all falls flat. Hāfez's language is far more nuanced than Omar Khayyam (d.1131) or Mowlavi (= Rumi, d.1273), and is untranslatable into other languages as poems. Commentaries about his poetry seem more feasible.

Hāfez's mastery in the way he uses language is unparalleled. He creates multiple layers of sensual metaphor like overlapping rose petals and holds them with sublime grace. Nothing is missing. When someone attempts to translate Hāfez's poem into another language, the most he can do is to grasp *one* of the petals; the poetic rhythm is lost, and so are the subtleties. It sounds like a cracked bell.

Hāfez (d.1390 AD), perhaps the most esoteric poet of Iran, is buried in Shiraz, Iran. According to a handwritten note found on Goethe's desk, Goethe considered himself an inspired disciple of Hāfez.

As an Iranian how can I learn more authentic Farsi words?

<u>For second-generation Iranians:</u> Whether you take a class or ask a native speaker to teach you Farsi, the key is to be aware and ask whether the word you're learning is Farsi or a hybrid mixed with Arabic. Your well-meaning friends may not be aware that what they teach you may not really be Farsi. Even the most basic verbs and daily exchanges such as *hello, how are you, happy birthday, goodbye, congratulations*, etc. are laced with Arabic. The good news is that by being alert you can learn Farsi correctly from the start.

<u>For first-generation Iranians:</u> If you are already fluent and can read/write in Farsi but would like to revive Farsi words in your life that are not Arabic-derived, there are many publications or online resources that give you Farsi equivalents. These are pages of translated words and say, for example, "Instead of khoda-Hāfez, say khodā-negáh-dār."

Here's a tip based on my personal experience (see section *In Search of Mother Tongue*). If you keep looking at the list and the two versions of the word, it'll be hard to forget the Arabic-derived one and learn the replacement. I suggest you write the replacement word (e.g. khodā-negáh-dār) on paper and later record it as voice memo in your phone. In other words, make yourself hear only the replacement word over and over until the old one eventually recedes. Start by replacing one phrase or word at a time and gradually feed it into your everyday speech. Be patient. It's easy to revert back to using the Arabic-derived word when we speak fast to each other. Don't give up.

The process I just described works for Farsi words that existed at one time but have been lost to Arabic. A more fundamental question is how can Farsi language grow and create *new* words so it can stay vital in the rapidly changing modern world. For example, how do we say "immunology, robot, highlighter, keyboard, skilled nursing facility" etc., in Farsi? If we keep switching to English words when we talk to each other, soon instead of losing Farsi to Arabic, we risk losing it to English.

Creating *new* words requires a systematic and analytical approach. There are scholars (see Heydari-Malayeri in Sources Consulted) who believe Farsi can have a bright future and create new words. Because Farsi is an Indo-European language, it can get help from its sister languages within the Indo-European family as well as from other Iranian languages spoken within Iran. It doesn't have to eclipse its future by remaining shackled to Arabic words that have flooded our language.

It's regrettable how we have allowed Arabic to intrude and penetrate our language and culture. It is not going to be productive to blame others. We need to wake up and take responsibility for freeing Farsi from this choke hold. It takes one person at a time and one word at a time. Farsi is not just a language. It is a key that opens the door to an entire realm of rich culture and history and wisdom that would otherwise remain inaccessible.

What is the *Order of Magi?* Is it the same as Mogh?
This question may be of more interest to students of Mazdaism.
Short answer: Magi (plural of Magavan) were initial supporters of Zártosht as mentioned in the *Gāthā*.
Moghs, on the other hand, are the groups that distorted Zártosht's message.

Longer answer: You may remember the word *Mogh* from an earlier discussion (see *Background in Reading the Gāthā section*). I discussed how *Moghs*, a powerful priestly clan, inserted many of their earlier Aryan (e.g. Mithraic) practices that Zártosht had strongly rejected, and presented their concoction as Zártosht's teachings.

Confusion comes from the word *Magavan* that appears a few times in the Gāthā (e.g., Gāt# 51/15 and #53/7). *Maga* in Sanskrit means reward, wealth, blessing. No one has related it to a secret society or rituals that induce a trance. Magavan in the Gāthā is similar to the Sanskrit word and ought to mean the *one who possesses Maga*.

Some scholars (e.g. Āzárgoshasb, Poordavood) correctly say that Magavan refers to a fellowship, order, or assembly of Zártosht's supporters (Magi is the plural). However, they mistakenly translate Magavan as Mogh. They say this brotherhood was instrumental in spreading Zártosht's message, therefore, the Moghs cannot be the ones who later distorted his teachings.

Based on my readings, the moghs who distorted Zártosht's message should not be confused with the Magavan mentioned in the Gāthā. Thus, translating Magavan as Mogh is not appropriate. I find using the word Magi confusing and prefer to use Mogh and Magavan, as needed.

Were Achaemenians Mázdean?

Short answer: Many authors claim that, but I think it depends on which Achaemenian ruler we're talking about.

Longer answer: At the time of Achaemenian dynasty, a thousand years had already passed and Zártosht's message had already deteriorated somewhat. Darius I's conduct and reign was most congruent with the spirit of Zártosht's message; Cyrus was also influenced by Zártosht but to a lesser degree. The original message of Zártosht deteriorates with passage of time.

Which dynasty was in power during the Alexander invasion, the Arab Conquest and the Mongol invasion?

Achaemenian   550-330 BC
   Alexander invasion   330–247 BC

Sassanian   224-651 AD
   Arab Conquest   637 AD

Kharazmian   1077-1231 AD
   Mongol Invasion   1220-1223 AD

SOURCES CONSULTED

(* Sources in Farsi)

*Ashtiani, J. (1989) *Zártosht: Mazdayasna va Hokoomat*. Enteshar Publisher: Tehran

*Āzárgoshasb, F. (1972) Vol I, II. *Gāthā: Soroodhāyeh Zártosht* [Gathas: Chants of Zártosht]. Foroohar Publications: Tehran.

*Āzárgoshasb, F. (1981) *Gāthā: Soroodhāyeh Asemani-e Zártosht* [Gathas: Sublime chants of Zoroaster]. Publisher unlisted.

Boyce, M. (1975-1982). *A history of Zoroastrianism* (Vol 1-2), Leiden: E. J. Brill.

*Dehkhoda, A. (2007) *Loghat Nāmé Dehkhoda*. 2 Vol. [Dehkhoda Encyclopedia]. Tehran University Press: Tehran

Dhalla, M. (1938) *History of Zoroastrianism*, New York

Edinger, E. (1984) *The Creation of Consciousness: Jung's Myth for Modern Man*. Inner City Books, Toronto

_____ (1985) *Anatomy of the Psyche: Alchemical Symbolism in Psychotherapy*. Open Court Publishing Company, La Salle, IL

_____ (1986) *The Bible and the Psyche, Individuation Symbolism in the Old Testament*. Inner City Books, Toronto

_____ (1986) *Encounter with the Self: A Jungian Commentary on William Blake's Illustrations of the Book of Job*. Inner City Books, Toronto.

_____ (1992) *Transformation of the God-Image: An Elucidation of Jung's Answer to Job.* Inner City Books, Toronto

_____ (1995) *The Mysterium Lectures: A Journey though C.G. Jung's Mysterium Coniunctionis.* Inner City Books, Toronto

Emerson, R. (1883) *Essays.* Houghton Mifflin Co., New York

*Ghaznavi M. and Ghani, Gh. (2017) *Divāné Hāfez* [The Complete GhaLzals of Hāfez]. Ibex Publishers: Maryland

Giles, L. (1925) *Taoist Teachings.* Translation from Lieh-tzu. Murray: London

Haug, M. *Essays on the sacred language, writing, and religions of the Parsis,* 1st ed., 1862, 3rd ed., London, 1884, repr. 1971

*Heydari-Malayeri, M. [YouTube], Includes many informative videos regarding Iranian languages, history, and culture of Iran.
https://Hāfez.youtube.com/channel/UCEk8n8sDATqDWjjI_jByKqQ/about

Jacobi, J. (1973) *The Psychology of C.G. Jung,* with a Foreword by C.G. Jung. Translated by Ralph Manheim. Yale University Press, Connecticut

Jonas, (1963) *The Gnostic Religion* (2nd ed., rev.). Beacon Press, Boston

Jung, C.G. *The Collected Works of CG Jung.* Princeton University Press, Princeton. (Bollingen Series XX); London: Routledge & Kegan Paul; especially the following:

  Vol. 5. Symbols of Transformation. 1956
  Vol. 7. Two Essays on Analytical Psychology. 1953

Vol. 8. The Structure and Dynamics of the Psyche, 1972
Vol. 9. Part I. The Archetypes and the Collective Unconscious, 1968
Vol. 11. Psychology and Religion: West and East. 1958
Vol. 12. Psychology and Alchemy. 2nd edn., rev., Princeton, 1968
Vol. 13. Alchemical Studies, 1968
Vol. 14. Mysterium Coniunctionis, 1965
Vol. 16 The Practice of Psychotherapy, 1966

____ (1973) *Letters*, Vol I, Ed. G. Adler, and A. Jaffe. Trans. R. F. C. Hull. Princeton University Press, Princeton, NJ

____ (1989) *Memories, Dreams and Reflections*. Vintage Books, New York

____ (2010) *Answer to Job*. Princeton University Press. Princeton, NJ

*Khazai, Kh. (2007) *The Gathas: The Sublime Book of Zarathustra*. European Center for Zoroastrian Studies, Brussels. (This is a small book in English.)

*Mehr, F. (1991) *The Zoroastrian Tradition: An Introduction to the Ancient Wisdom of Zarathustra*. Element, Inc., Massachusetts

Mills, L. (2010) *A study of the five Zoroastrian Gāthās*. Kessinger Publishing, Montana

*Natel-Khānlari, P. (1995) *Tārikhé Zabāné Farsi* [The history of Farsi language], 3, Vols. Simurgh Publisher, Tehran

Neumann, E. (1973) *The Origins and History of Consciousness*. Princeton University Press, Princeton. (Bollingen Series XLII)

*Poordavood, E. (2010) *The Gāthā: Oldest parts of Avesta*. Asāteer Publishing, Tehran

Rilke, R. (1996) *Rilke's book of hours: Love Poems to God*. Translated by Anita Barrows and Joanna Macey. Riverhead Books, New York

Romanyshyn, R. (1989) *Technology as Symptom and Dream*. Routledge, New York

Samuels, A. (1986). *A critical dictionary of Jungian analysis*. London and New York: Routledge and Kegan Paul

Taraporewala, I.J.S. (1980) *Religion of Zarathustra*. Sazman-E-Faravahar Publishing, Tehran

Watts, A. (1955) *The Way of Liberation in Zen Buddhism*. American Academy of Asian Studies, San Francisco

_____ (1957) *The Way of Zen*. Vintage Books, NY

Whitmont, E.C. (1969) *The Symbolic Quest*. Princeton University Press, Princeton, NJ

Wilhelm, R. (1962) *The Secret of the Golden Flower*. A Chinese Book of Life, with a Commentary by C.G. Jung. Harcourt Brace Jovanovich, NY

_____ (1950) *The I Ching or Book of Changes*. 2 vols. Translated by Cary Baynes, Pantheon, NY

Ancient Pearls of Wisdom

*Learning the Language
of Inner Voice*

by Azarm Ghareman, PhD

Available in Paperback and eBook

Find a link to purchase at

https://mazdaconnections.com

Made in the USA
Middletown, DE
19 June 2024